MIRACLE OF THE HEARTBEAT

GOD'S GIFT OF TIME - OVER 23 MILLION ADDED SECONDS

Sandra Colvard Ray

Copyright © 2024 Sandra Colvard Ray.

All rights reserved. No part of this book may be used or reproduced by any means, graphic, electronic, or mechanical, including photocopying, recording, taping or by any information storage retrieval system without the written permission of the author except in the case of brief quotations embodied in critical articles and reviews.

This book is a work of non-fiction. Unless otherwise noted, the author and the publisher make no explicit guarantees as to the accuracy of the information contained in this book and in some cases, names of people and places have been altered to protect their privacy.

WestBow Press books may be ordered through booksellers or by contacting:

WestBow Press
A Division of Thomas Nelson & Zondervan
1663 Liberty Drive
Bloomington, IN 47403
www.westbowpress.com
844-714-3454

Because of the dynamic nature of the Internet, any web addresses or links contained in this book may have changed since publication and may no longer be valid. The views expressed in this work are solely those of the author and do not necessarily reflect the views of the publisher, and the publisher hereby disclaims any responsibility for them.

Any people depicted in stock imagery provided by Getty Images are models, and such images are being used for illustrative purposes only.
Certain stock imagery © Getty Images.

ISBN: 979-8-3850-2822-1 (sc)
ISBN: 979-8-3850-2823-8 (e)

Library of Congress Control Number: 2024912594

Print information available on the last page.

WestBow Press rev. date: 08/06/2024

CONTENTS

Chapter 1   The Road to the Diagnosis 1
Chapter 2   What Do We Do Now? 10
Chapter 3   When It Rains... It Pours 13
Chapter 4   A Funeral and When the Hospital Became our Home.... 16
Chapter 5   God, Please Give Me the Words 20
Chapter 6   New Challenges................................. 26
Chapter 7   Now We Wait................................. 28
Chapter 8   When Heartache Came Knocking Again 31
Chapter 9   When God Showed up in a Mighty Way 36
Chapter 10 The Transplant 39
Chapter 11 Going Home................................. 44
Chapter 12 Stem Cell Transplant 50
Chapter 13 Going Home, Again 58
Chapter 14 When August Came 61
Chapter 15 The Day that Changed Everything................................. 65
Chapter 16 Going Home –Without Tom 70
Chapter 17 The Autopsy 72
Reflections................................. 75

Dear Reader,

It has been over twenty years since his death, and I now feel that I can tell this story. I feel that God had urged me to finish this story for three reasons – one, so others will understand this rare disease and the importance of organ transplantation, two, so that people will know the man who had the courage and bravery to fight against its ravages with more grace and dignity than humanly possible, and finally, but most importantly, so that others can know that even when everything in life that happens is not good, God himself is inherently good and pours his goodness into our lives even amidst the most difficult circumstances. I started this story four years after Tom's death. It has taken me 17 years to complete it, as over the years, every time I sat down and worked on the next part of the story, I would write some and then stop. The memories, the pain, the trauma of it all came flooding back to my very core. If I worked more than a day or two, I would start having nightmares again and go back into the deep state of depression that was once my reality. So, I would put it aside and force it from my mind so that I would not have to feel the pain all over again. I doubted that I would ever finish this story. I felt no urgency or desire to even complete it. However, one day as I was looking for some photos on an old flash drive, this story jumped out at me. It had been a few years since I had written anything on it. As I closed my computer, I heard a still small voice inside of me saying that I needed to finish it. My first thought was that I did not want to go there. I did not want to relive the pain of those years. God quickly changed my thoughts and reminded me that I had a story of his love and goodness to share with others. I was a personal witness to many miracles that God performed and not to share and give God his due glory for them was a sin of omission on my part. My thoughts were further confirmed during a sermon at church the next week. Our pastor spoke about turning our pain into a sacrifice of praise and how God can handle our pain and use our pain to help someone else. For the first time since I started writing this story, I felt an urgency to finish it. There are so many people hurting from life events that threaten to overwhelm them and could benefit from reading about how God shows up even in the hardest of times.

I feel that this story is meant to be told at this point in history, and

God has a plan for someone who will read it. Tom would tell everyone that the most important change in his life began at the point when he made the decision to go to the altar at our church and surrender all to Christ in the year 2000. This decision changed his life, his priorities and how he lived the remainder of his life. Looking back now, I see this year as a pivotal year – a year when we were made truly aware of the love and forgiving grace of God and the words of John 3:16. Little did either of us know how crucial the faith-building year of 2000 would become in our lives when, in 2002, Tom would be diagnosed with an incurable and rare illness. He once said that if everything that he went through helped lead one person to Christ, then it was all worth it. Tom's strong faith and belief has impacted more lives than he could have ever realized and although twenty years have passed, there remains an ongoing impact from Tom's life multiplied through each of those lives. If putting this story on paper so that others can read it does the same, then I will know my purpose for completing it. Even now, as I finish up the end of our story, the pain, the tears and the memories are often too much to bear, and I stop and come back another time. Although the pain will never completely leave me and these memories are still very vivid in my mind, I am thankful that God allowed me the strength to put these words on paper so that others may understand the man, the disease and the power of God's love and grace. Some of you may be fighting the same disease that was Tom's diagnosis or other diseases that are just as difficult. For you and those who love you, I pray that when you need it most, you will find strength from the hope and promises found in the 23rd Psalm and in John 3:16.

– Sandra

CHAPTER 1

THE ROAD TO THE DIAGNOSIS

It all started in November of 2001. My husband, Tom, started having pain and numbness in his legs and feet. Often, he would awaken at night and complain of pain shooting down his legs. I remember him describing it as if there was something on fire in his lower legs, and it was trying to get out the bottom of his feet. He went to see his family doctor about this, and the doctor felt as if there was some pressure being put on the nerves in his legs and it was probably back related. Tom's father had a history of back problems and suffered with spinal stenosis, a condition due to narrowing of the spinal cord causing nerve pinching which leads to persistent pain, lack of feeling in the lower extremities, and decreased physical activity. Since Tom's symptoms seemed so similar, we all felt this was a likely diagnosis, and we scheduled an appointment with the same neurosurgeon that his father had been seeing for his condition. The doctor scheduled an MRI, and we fully expected the results to be as we thought. He would have spinal stenosis, therefore, causing all the discomfort he was experiencing in his lower extremities, and we would look at the different treatment options available. We were surprised when only some very mild stenosis showed up, and the doctor assured us that it was not severe enough to cause the leg pain that Tom was experiencing.

We were back to square one, and he was still in a great deal of pain.

Tom had started a regular daily work-out routine at our local gym several months prior to this. Since the MRI showed nothing to be concerned about, the doctor discussed his work-out routine and together they felt that maybe he had been going too hard at it and had put some pressure on the nerves causing some of his discomfort. He gave him some pills for the pain and asked him to take it a little easier in the gym. He told him to come back if he soon did not see an improvement. Soon after this, I started noticing other symptoms. When Tom came home from work, he would seem unusually tired. Tom was always full of energy and life. He helped with dinner, dishes, laundry, the children and anything that needed to be done around the house. He never sat down to watch TV or rest until the chores were done and we both could sit down together. Suddenly, he would have the need to sit down after dinner and then quickly fall asleep. It was a shock to me to see him going to bed around 8:00 some nights. I encouraged him to call the doctor back and explain that he was not getting any better. He was still having the problem with the pain and numbness in his legs and now in his fingers as well. Another thing I noticed was that he was losing weight. I talked with him about his workouts and thought that he was still going overboard with them. All of this was going on around the holidays, and Tom was just trying to get through Christmas and was convinced that he could fix his problem if he would just get a handle on his workouts. He felt he must be doing something wrong in his weightlifting that was still creating problems with his back and causing his continued discomfort. I, on the other hand, was not so sure. His weight loss and lack of energy concerned me, and I begged him to call the doctor back. We were scheduled to go to the beach over a weekend in January with friends and he assured me that he would call when we got back. While we were at the beach, a new symptom developed. One night while we were playing cards with our friends, he put his ankles up on a chair, and we all gasped as we noticed that his ankles were swollen with fluid. I was now convinced that something was terribly wrong, and as soon as we returned home, he called the doctor back. He explained that his symptoms had not improved; they had worsened. Since this doctor was a neurosurgeon that specializes in back-related issues, he did not feel as if there was anything further he could do to help Tom. Since the majority of his symptoms seemed nerve related, he referred him to a neurologist. The earliest appointment we could get was in March of 2002. With that being over a month and half away, we had no choice but to wait and hope his condition did not get worse. However, things became progressively worse. When he walked up the stairs at night to tuck our 7-year-old son into bed, he would have to stop at the top of the stairs to catch his breath before continuing down the hall. Doing simple things like throwing a baseball, or mowing the grass exhausted him so much that he would have to quit. He was still going to work; however, when he returned home each day, he was so tired that he was ready to go to bed. The numbness and pain that he was having was growing in intensity. Finally, it was time to go to the specialist. I was relieved that we were going to get a diagnosis and get him some help.

I will never forget that day. We drove an hour and a half from our home and walked into the doctor's office. The doctor asked him, "What seems to be the problem today?"

Tom told him, "I have felt so bad that I just wanted to put myself into an ambulance and check into a hospital somewhere."

The doctor's reply to that was, "They would not have put you in the hospital; you don't even look sick." I immediately saw Tom drop his head, and a look of defeat fell across his face. I could tell he was thinking, "Maybe all of this is just in my head. Maybe, I am not really sick." After a brief examination, the doctor told him that he thought he had peripheral neuropathy. This condition can cause temporary numbness, tingling, and pricking sensations, sensitivity to touch, or muscle weakness. It can also cause burning pain, especially at night. This would explain why he was having the pain and numbness in his arms and legs. He told him that a lot of people have this and are in worse shape than he was, and basically that he would just have to live with it. He thought it was probably idiopathic neuropathy, which does not have a specific cause; however, he would run a couple of tests to make sure it was not coming from diabetes or some other major cause. We felt some relief that this was all it was, and it was nothing life threatening. However, I could not shake the fact he was ignoring a lot of other symptoms. I remember saying to this doctor, "What about his weight loss, the shortness of breath? I tried to stress to the doctor how I had watched his condition deteriorate quickly over the last two months. I really felt in my gut that something was seriously wrong. He brushed off what I was saying as if I were an overprotective and paranoid wife who really did not know what I was talking about. He gave the impression that he was the doctor, and if he did not feel it was anything serious, then I should not worry so much. He prescribed him some medication and sent us home.

We waited patiently over the next couple of weeks to hear the results of the tests the doctor had performed. He showed no signs of diabetes, which is the leading cause of peripheral neuropathy. He was clear of any infections or auto-immune disorders that can cause neuropathies. Nothing showed on the tests that were performed that alarmed the doctor of any serious illness. He was told by the nurse that called him that the "doctor wanted him to sit tight and call back in four months if he was still having problems." By this time, Tom was really feeling like his symptoms must be in his head. I recall him telling me that he was just going to have to toughen up and get over it.

I could not accept this and decided to find another doctor that specialized in peripheral neuropathy. Through an online search, I located a doctor at Duke Medical Center in Durham. He had an impressive resume and neuropathies were his specialty. I called the next day and scheduled an appointment. The first available appointment was in late April. Although this was three weeks away, we took it and hoped to find a more caring doctor who would dig deeper into his symptoms. Over this three-week period, he continued to grow weaker, and doing things that required much movement was out of the question. When we arrived at the office, the doctor sat down and listened intently to our story from the first symptom to the last. When we described how out of breath and weak he had become when doing simple tasks, he had Tom lie down on a table and he took his blood pressure. He had him immediately stand up and he took it again. It dropped 30 points from the resting position to the standing position. I could see from the look on the doctor's face that this concerned him. Next, he ordered a chest x-ray. Since we had driven three and half hours to the appointment, we waited at the hospital for the results of the x-ray. When the doctor returned to the small room we were waiting in, I noticed the look on his face was one of great apprehension. He told us that he felt Tom had one of two things, either cancer of the nerves, which is extremely rare, or a disease called amyloidosis, which is even rarer. Since I had never even heard of the word, amyloidosis, I immediately felt it must be cancer. I sat there in disbelief, my mind in a whirlwind as to what this would mean to battle cancer of this sort. Then the doctor said that he felt like amyloidosis was a more likely finding because Tom's heart was enlarged. I was full of questions: "What is amyloidosis? What does it mean to have an enlarged heart? How was this enlarged heart related to pain and numbness in his legs and hands?" Before we got too concerned, the doctor wanted to run the proper tests to see if his theory was correct. We were told he would need to check into the hospital, and they would have to do a biopsy of a nerve and of his heart. These seemed to be the two major areas that were being affected. We went home that day, and I immediately sat down at the computer and started reading everything I could find about this disease that had totally baffled us. I found out that amyloidosis occurs when plasma cells in bone marrow produce proteins that misfold and deposit in tissues, leading to organ failure and death. I also read that in the United States, there are approximately 3000 new cases per year, although researchers believe the disease is highly underdiagnosed.

I sat at the computer, and tears ran down my face as I realized that it was a fatal disease that had no known cause or treatment. Although the symptoms of some types can be controlled for a time, the eventual result was death. A few hours earlier, I thought that cancer was the worst thing we would have to battle. This seemed even worse. We checked into the hospital a couple of days later, and they performed the biopsies. I learned that amyloidosis can only be diagnosed by a positive biopsy; that is, an identification of the amyloid deposits in a piece of tissue. Tissue biopsies must be stained properly with Congo red, a dye which will color the amyloid if it is present and cause it to have a unique appearance when viewed under a special microscope. We waited patiently for the results, praying that they would be negative, and he would not have this awful disease. I remember sitting on the edge of his bed when a team of doctors entered the room. The look on their faces told the entire story. The doctor who had been so caring and listened to our complaints simply nodded his head up and down and spoke as if a definite lump had settled in his throat. "It's positive," he said. Amyloidosis had attacked Tom's heart and nervous system. They went on to explain that his heart was too weak for their hospital to consider doing a stem cell transplant, nor did they have any other avenues for treatment. Six months to live was the best option they gave us. At that moment, our world fell apart. One minute we were an ordinary family living an ordinary life, and now suddenly, we were faced with a terminal disease that would alter our ordinary lives forever. I broke down and started crying, trying to will my mind into believing what we had just been told.

As I lay down across Tom's chest and cried, he simply ran his fingers through my hair, and said, "Don't worry, it will be OK." The doctors left the room, giving us time to digest the news. They told us they would be back later to discuss the next step as to how we would proceed from here. Later, I was told that this disease was so rare that the doctors were not even sure themselves which path to take. I think they needed time to investigate possibilities that were out there for amyloidosis patients.

Later in the day, they came back in and told us about the Amyloid Treatment and Research Center at Boston University. They were one of the top research and treatment centers in the United States. They recommended that we travel there and let them evaluate Tom's situation for possible treatment. They set everything up with the center and explained to us that Tom's best chance of survival was to have a stem cell transplant. Even though Duke did not feel as if they would be able to perform the transplant, this treatment center specialized in the treatment of amyloid patients and doing stem cell transplants was a routine procedure for them. Suddenly we were feeling some hope where just a few hours before there was none. Stem cell transplant and high dose chemotherapy was the most aggressive treatment to date for amyloidosis. We were told that if he qualified for this type of treatment then we would have to stay in Boston for six to eight weeks while he underwent his treatment. I was a teacher, and school was almost out for the summer. I took the remaining couple of weeks off and we started preparing for a long summer in Boston. Our seven-year-old son, Troy, would spend the summer with his grandparents, and our prayer was to go and get this nightmare behind us and be back in time for the new school year to start in August. My oldest son, Brent, was already out of school and in college, so knowing he was situated was one less worry I had.

We left for Boston on June 1st, four days before Tom's 46th birthday. The trip itself was exhausting for him. He slept much of the way on the plane, and when we landed, he was unable to walk through the airport. I had to get him a wheelchair. Walking any distance put him completely out of breath. We took a cab to our hotel, and I got him settled in and went out to find us some dinner. By this point, going out for dinner was a thing of the past. The tasks of everyday life were becoming extremely difficult for Tom. I was afraid to leave him in the room alone for very long. I was scared he would pass out or his heart would stop beating. I quickly picked up some sandwiches from a shop down in the lobby, and I went back upstairs where I found him fast asleep. I sat there and watched him sleep and started to cry. I was terrified of the sudden changes I was seeing in my husband, and still today as I write this many years later, the fear still grips me deep inside. I guess it will never leave. I pray often that it will, but it still lives very real inside of me. I know this because every time I sit down at my computer to work on this story, the tears start flowing freely, and I have not even gotten to the hard part yet. Sometimes I think I cannot do this; I cannot write this; it still hurts too much; but I know that I must tell his story.

The next morning, we went to Boston Medical Center with high hopes of finally putting this disease in remission and moving on with our lives. Tom was a manager at our local telephone company. It was a job that he loved dearly, and he looked forward to getting back to work. He would undergo a three-day outpatient evaluation consisting of several tests and consultations which would help determine his amyloid type and organ system involvement. Once the evaluation was complete, a treatment plan would be recommended. We were guided through each step of the evaluation, and the doctors and nurses explained why each test was being done and what the results meant. Another shock to us was to find out that there is more than one type of amyloidosis. There is primary, secondary and hereditary. One of the tests they would run would be to determine which type Tom had. The word hereditary sent even more panic through us, thinking that if he had this type then our son may also be destined to one day face this disease. While Tom spent the next three days being evaluated, I was going through real estate brochures trying to find us a place to rent for the next two months while he underwent his treatment. All treatment was done on an outpatient basis, and we would not be able to afford to stay in a hotel for six or eight weeks.

On the third day, after being seen by cardiologist, hematologist, and neurologist, the head cardiologist sat us down to discuss their findings.

Fully expecting him to share an outline for Tom's stem cell procedure and course of treatment, we were again devastated when he looked at us and said, "I'm sorry, there is nothing we can do, it has progressed too far, your heart is already stiff with amyloid deposits, it could never withstand a stem cell transplant. If we would have seen you sooner than we probably could have helped you." Tom and I sat there not knowing what to say. Finally, Tom asks, "Now what do I do?"

With a dismal look on his face, the doctor stated, "Go home and get your affairs in order, you probably have at best 3 to 6 months to live." This was not what we came to Boston to hear. We had come to this specialized treatment center, with suitcases full of clothes, expecting to be here for the summer. This was our last hope and the end of any possibility of getting Tom a stem cell transplant to slow down this aggressive disease. I had been convinced that since we were able to get in at one of the top hospitals in the country that treat this disease, with doctors that knew all about it, that they would be able to help us. It never occurred to me that we would be turned away. I asked the doctor for more clarification, as I did not want to digest what he was saying. He explained that they caught it too late, it had progressed too far. My mind drifted back to the doctor we saw in March who so easily dismissed Tom and his symptoms. What if he had ordered a chest x-ray or checked his blood pressure in different positions like the doctor at Duke did? I asked the cardiologist sitting before us if we had come in March instead of June, would it have made a difference? He stated that it would be hard to know for sure, but three months earlier the amyloid would not have been as built up on his heart, and they probably would have been able to do the stem cell transplant.

Regret, remorse, and anger, mixed with sadness swept over me. At that moment, I wanted to go back in time and beg and plead with the doctor, who made Tom feel as if he would just have to learn to live with neuropathy, to listen to us. I knew then that something was terribly wrong with Tom, but I could not get him to take us seriously. What a difference three months may have made. If there was one bright spot in any of the information he gave us, it was that he did not have hereditary amyloidosis. There was no danger of it being passed on to our son. We went back to our hotel, neither of us knowing what to say. As always, Tom was the strong one. He was just so grateful that Troy would never inherit the disease. We packed our bags and took the next flight home.

We had planned to stay all summer and beat this disease, but we were going home in less than a week of arriving, with a death sentence hanging over our heads. "How were we going to tell the boys, his parents, and my family? How do you face knowing that at age 46 you may have three months to live?"

CHAPTER 2

WHAT DO WE DO NOW?

When we returned home, I remember driving up our driveway and looking at our home with its wrap-around porch and swing set in the yard; the house that Tom and I had planned and where we had built our lives as a family for 14 years. If only today were an ordinary day when Tom and I could enjoy sitting on the porch and watching Troy swing, instead of this day, when we were facing the fact that we had only three months together, and nothing would ever be the same again. I dreaded more than anything having to explain to our young son that his father only had a short time to live and there seemed to be nothing we could do about it. While in Boston, we had asked a counselor about what the best way was to handle explaining this to a child. He told us that a moment would happen in conversation, and we would know when it was right to tell him. Over the next couple of days that moment came. One night as Troy was preparing to get into the shower, he told his dad that he would be glad when this amyloidosis was over, and he could throw the ball with him again. I was sitting in the bedroom on the bed folding clothes, and I heard the conversation through the door. I instinctively knew that the moment had come, and Tom would seize this opportunity to tell him.

My eyes started flooding with tears as I knew what words were about to come from Tom's mouth. He said, "Son, Daddy may not get better from this amyloidosis, at least not on this earth. Sometimes, God takes us to heaven to be able to heal us and that may be what God has planned for Daddy."

By this point, my heart was completely breaking as I imagined that my son would start screaming and crying upon hearing this news. Instead, he very calmly says, "Daddy, have you read James, chapter 5?"

Tom replies, "Yes, I have."

Troy then asks, "Well, have you done what it says?"

Tom replies, "No, I have not."

As he steps in the shower, Troy tells him, "Daddy, when I get out of this shower, you and I are going to read James chapter 5 and then we are going to pray about this." Tom then walks into the bedroom, where I am still sitting on the bed, sits down with me and we stare at each other, albeit through blinding tears, in total amazement at the words that have come from Troy's mouth. Immediately I thought of the verse in the Bible about having the faith of a child and realized that my seven-year-old son had more faith than I. Here we were, ready to give up completely because of a doctor's diagnosis and Troy's first thought was to turn to the Bible for the answers. When he got out of the shower, he and Tom sat down and read James chapter 5, focusing on verses 13 and 14. "Is any among you afflicted? Let him pray. Is any merry? Let him sing. Is any sick among you? Let him call for the elders of the church; and let them pray over him, anointing him with oil in the name of the Lord." Tom promised Troy that the next day he would call our pastor and set this up with the deacons of our church. Hearing this was all the comfort that Troy seemed to need. He went on to bed and rested peacefully through the night. I knew that my biggest concern was in God's control, and he had already put a hedge of protection and peace around my son.

It is hard to explain the fire that Troy's words lit under me that night. I knew that I had to put my total trust in God with Tom's health and instead of accepting the three-month death sentence, I had to get busy looking for other avenues to help him. Since the doctor had explained that his heart was already too weak to withstand a stem cell transplant, my logic was to get him a heart transplant first and with the new heart then he could withstand the stem cell transplant that could possibly save or at least prolong his life. I called the doctors back at Boston University to ask them about this possibility. They explained to me that the chances of him ever getting on a heart transplant list were less than 1%. He stated that no medical center would risk giving a person with amyloidosis a new heart as the amyloid would just attack the new heart as well. Once again, I felt all the hope of helping Tom slip away. To combat the feeling of hopelessness, I continued to research hospitals that performed heart transplants and inquired about the possibility of getting him on the donor list. My requests were denied over and over as soon as they found out he had amyloidosis. Looking back now, I remember how well Tom took all this news. While I continued to search and plead with determination to find someone who would help him, he was accepting the fact that his time was short, and he needed to get his affairs in order. He did contact our pastor and had our deacons pray over him. He did have faith that God was going to heal him of this dreadful disease; however, he knew that this meant his healing may come in the form of death from this life and receiving a new glorified body in Jesus Christ. He had accepted this to the point that he had the funeral director from our local funeral home come to our house, and he planned his entire funeral with him. He planned everything, right down to the music. He told me that he did not want me to have to worry about it when he passed away. I remember being angry at him for doing this, because in my eyes, he was giving up. He was admitting defeat, and I did not want any part of it. I did not find it in me to go sit down at the table with him when he was planning with the director; instead, I just walked around the outside of my house and cried, "God, how can this be happening?"

CHAPTER 3

WHEN IT RAINS...
IT POURS

As we continued moving into July and then August, I knew that time was slipping through my fingers to find someone who would be willing to help Tom. Our three-month death sentence was fast approaching. Each day, I watched as more life was taken from him. He was sleeping more than ever, his breathing was more labored, fluid was building up in his abdomen and legs, and he could only take a few steps without having to sit down and rest. Cardiac amyloidosis changes the structure of the heart. As amyloid proteins build up on the heart muscles, the walls of the heart thicken, and the heart enlarges. Over time, the heart struggles to pump, therefore becoming weak and eventually leading to congestive heart failure. Due to this heart failure, Tom had excessive fluid accumulation throughout his body. Many times, we ended up at our family doctor's office to have Lasix injections to treat the accumulation. Meanwhile, I was still calling hospitals and doctors, trying to find someone who would be willing to put him on a heart transplant list. My efforts continued to hit dead ends as no one would even consider putting an amyloid patient on the transplant list. Outside of trying to help Tom, I was dealing with an additional crisis. My 87-year-old father, who I loved more than life, had been placed in the hospital and was not doing well. I would have one of Tom's parents come to the house to sit with him while

I could go visit. My heart was double breaking as I was watching the life drain from my father and husband at the same time. Even as I write these words, I remember how I had to call out for God to give me the strength to stay strong while I dealt with the possibility of losing the two most important men in my life.

On August 26th, Tom was having even more difficulty breathing and couldn't walk more than 10 feet, before he would become so short of breath that he would have to stop. We went back to the family doctor as we knew the fluid was building back up in his system. His doctor told him that he felt he needed to send him to Baptist Hospital in Winston Salem. We lived in the mountains of North Carolina and our small-town hospital was not equipped to handle Tom's condition and the fluid was accumulating faster than he could take care of it. When we arrived at the hospital, Tom was admitted into the Coronary Care Unit (CCU) where they gave him an infusion of Natrecor, which greatly improved his symptoms. Once stabilized, they were able to transfer him out of CCU onto the cardiac floor where he was closely monitored throughout the remainder of his time in the hospital. His baseline function improved, and we were able to go home on August 30th. Although we had been cleared to go home, I could not help but wonder how long it would be until the fluid built back up in his system and we would be right back at the hospital.

As we moved into September, things were critical for my father and despite having just come from a hospital stay, Tom was already starting to feel poorly again. I felt helpless, powerless and at a complete loss. I have always been a "fix-it" type person, and what was happening around me was completely out of my control and my world was quickly unraveling.

Then on September 4th, my oldest sister called and said, "Sandra, you need to come to the hospital. Daddy is dying."

I quickly called for one of Tom's parents to come and stay with him. I jumped in the car and raced to the hospital. Luckily, we only lived about five miles away, and I prayed the whole way to make it in time. I was driving about 70 miles per hour in a 45 zone, but I didn't care. I had to see my daddy and tell him goodbye. I arrived at the hospital and went to the second floor to his room. I am the youngest of five siblings, and the others were there gathered around him. When I walked in the room, they all looked at me. My oldest sister looked sadly at me and shook her head. I did not make it. He was gone!

"No," I screamed! I had to say goodbye. I had to see him one last time. I guess it was from the stress of Tom's illness and now this, but I collapsed to the floor. My siblings were quickly around me and picked me up. We all just sat there and cried together. All our hearts were broken, but I also knew that my siblings were even more concerned for me and what I was going through in addition to our father's death. Being the youngest of the five, I have always felt the protection of my siblings like an umbrella hovering above my head. We had lost our precious father, the man we all looked up to and who had influenced our beliefs, morals, and character. Our world was changed forever.

Eventually, I went back home knowing I was now faced with sharing this sad news with Tom. He too loved Daddy and would be devastated by his loss. I walked in the door to find Tom sitting up in his recliner and knew that it had taken every ounce of his strength to be up waiting for me to return. These days, he was primarily confined to the bed as sitting up took too much of his energy and breath. He took one look at my face and knew. He asked me if I made it in time. I quietly shook my head no. Tears ran down his face as he used his weak breath to tell me how sorry he was. He blamed himself that I was not there in my daddy's last moments. He said, "If you had not had to be here taking care of me, then you would have been there." I told him that it was not his fault, and I was exactly where I needed to be. I sat down on the floor beside his recliner and just cried, letting out all my pain and frustration. Tom gently rubbed my hair and as always became the one trying to comfort me even though he was the one in terrible pain and facing death's seemingly open door.

CHAPTER 4

A FUNERAL AND WHEN THE HOSPITAL BECAME OUR HOME

On September 5, one day after my father's death, Tom collapsed. His breathing was shallow, and I knew the fluid had built steadily back in his lungs. We rushed him back to our doctor's office. By now, we had become accustomed to just coming through the back door to see him whenever things got bad. After what had happened on August 26th, I knew that he would be immediately sent back to Baptist Hospital. My thoughts were confirmed when our doctor called for a helicopter to pick him up and transport him to Winston Salem. I had planned to spend part of the day with my family planning my father's funeral. I needed to be with them and be a part of this to help with my own grieving. Instead, I was now quickly throwing necessary items in a bag and preparing myself for the hour and half ride to Winston Salem. As I drove down, what seemed like an endless road, to Winston Salem, I prayed to God to please not let me lose my father and husband in a two-day span. I'm not sure how I even made it safely there, driving through the constant flow of tears that kept pouring down my face. Since Tom had gone by helicopter, he would make it down at least an hour before I did. My thoughts kept urging me to go even faster because if I didn't, then Tom may also pass away before I could get to the hospital. Could I really be living this same nightmare twice? Tom was immediately admitted and placed back into the Cardiac Care Unit with severe congestive heart failure. We were told that the only thing they could do was to try and keep the fluid off his heart and out of his lungs with their goal being to just try and make him as comfortable as possible.

Over the next couple of days, various doctors from many departments came in and out of his room. Amyloidosis is a very rare disease and can affect any organ in the body in which it decides to deposit. Although this is one of the largest hospitals in North Carolina, they still were not used to seeing a patient with amyloidosis. Tom quickly became a case study from which everyone could learn. He was now hooked up to machines that would do for him what his heart was no longer able to handle. Fluid was being continually drained as it would build up, and a machine was helping his heart pump the blood through his body. It was obvious the end was near, and it was only a matter of time before the machines would no longer work as well. A team of cardiologists and neurologists started working together to determine what would be the course of action for Tom's care while he was in CCU. During these first two days, I had to return home to attend my father's funeral. I was scared to leave Tom, even for a minute, as I was anxious he would pass away, and I would not be there. However, I needed to go home to give my daddy a proper goodbye and be with my family. My heart was ripped. If only I could be in two places at once. This was not the last time I would feel this over the next few months. Through his weak breath, Tom urged me to go home and attend the funeral. He assured me that he would be there when I got back. As I was leaving him to start the drive back, the one thing he was sorry about was that he wouldn't be there at the funeral to support me. He squeezed my hand, made me promise to drive carefully and told me he would be there with me in love and spirit. As usual, the tears that ran down his face were not for himself but for me.

My mother, five siblings, their spouses, and all our children formed a long line at my father's visitation. Being the youngest, I was at the end of the line. I missed having Tom standing there beside me. Brent came home from college and became a source of strength for Troy and me. Troy was only 8 at this time, and I was additionally concerned at the toll that his grandfather's death and worrying about his own father was taking. In a matter of months, his intact family had fallen apart. His older brother had gone off to college, his father was handed a death sentence, his grandfather had passed away, and his mother was not at home. This was a tremendous load for anyone to deal with but especially an eight-year-old child. I was so thankful that both Troy and I had Brent there with us. He had grown into such a responsible young man, and his strength and support helped me get through what was, at this point, the worst day of my life. After the visitation, we prepared for the funeral. I remember sitting there listening to the wonderful stories being told about my sweet daddy. He was an amazing man who had lived a very hard life but handled it with grace and dignity. We all laughed and cried listening to these stories as we reflected on the man that had so greatly impacted all our lives. During the funeral, Troy was very clingy to me. I knew he was a scared little boy and was not sure how to process all that was going on in his world. I added this to the list of things that were breaking my heart and wondered just how much more I could possibly carry. I also noticed, as he was leaning against me, that he felt very warm. He seemed to be burning up with a fever. We got through the funeral and the graveside service. By the end of it, I could tell that Troy was very sick. I had originally planned to leave after the funeral to get back to Tom at the hospital. Instead, I knew that I had to get Troy checked to see what was going on with him. I rushed him to our local hospital's emergency room. By this time, I really was starting to feel like Job in the Bible. "God, how much more can I take?"

I just buried my father, I need to get back to Tom before he passes away, and now Troy is burning up with fever. Troy was diagnosed with double ear infections. I had the prescription for his medicine filled and took him back to his grandparents' house. He would continue to stay with them while I went back to Winston to be with Tom. Troy did not want me to leave him. He was sick and needed his mama. "Again, can I please be in two places at once? I wanted to stay there and comfort my son. I wanted to assure him that everything was going to be OK. I wanted to wake up from this continual nightmare that was becoming my life. I didn't want to admit the fact to him or even myself that I had to get back to the hospital to face yet another death. I left him in tears and tried to reassure him the best I could. I once again drove the long road to Winston Salem unsure of what I was going to have to face when I got there.

I returned to the hospital and found Tom as I had left him. I was thankful that he had not passed while I was gone. That was so very important to me; I did not want to lose him, but if he had to die, then I wanted to be beside him when it happened. I checked myself into a hotel that was across the street from the hospital. I would sit with Tom all day watching the machines do the work that his body was no longer able to perform. We would talk when he was able. He was so weak that he mostly just slept. The moments he was awake became cherished as I knew they would soon be gone. Tom was always so worried about me. I was there to try and keep his spirits up; after all he was the one who was basically tied to machines and feeling his life slip from him. However, he never wanted to talk about him. He used his energy to let me know what he wanted me to do in the future. He would tell me that he was fine because he would win either way. He stated that if God took him home and healed his body that he would be so happy and at peace there, or if God decided to heal him here on earth, then he would get to stay here with me and the rest of the family. He would say, "See, I win either way, but it's you I am worried about." I would paste on a smile while a tear ran down my face trying to be bold and not let him see just how much I was crumbling inside. I knew I had to stay strong for him, and I still was not ready to give up on my vision of getting him a new heart so that he could withstand the stem cell transplant he needed to help put this horrible disease in remission. There is no cure for amyloidosis; however, with a stem cell transplant it can be put in remission and slowed down. This would allow him to live longer. That was my goal. Troy was only 8 and needed a few more years with his father. I knew that I had to give my idea one last try.

CHAPTER 5

GOD, PLEASE GIVE ME THE WORDS

When I went back to the hotel one night, I got down on my knees and prayed as usual. Only this time, I really cried out to God. It was an urgent cry, a cry of desperation like I had never had before. I begged and pleaded with God to save Tom, to give us just a little more time. I knew we were down to the wire, and the machines would soon not be enough to keep him alive. He was in the Critical Care Unit, which is only reserved for the very worst patients, and they could not just keep him there indefinitely. Decisions would have to be made. "God, what do I do?" Show me the way; show me whether to let him go or continue the fight. I felt an overwhelming voice in my soul telling me to tell the doctors my plan that I had been trying to sell for the last two months to any doctor or hospital that would listen to me. No, that cannot be right, I thought. I had already contacted Baptist Hospital about putting him on a transplant list and was instantly turned down. They had only been doing heart transplants at the facility for around ten years and were working to build their program. They would not put an amyloid patient on the list and risk giving a heart to someone with no guarantee that the new heart would not be attacked as well. I gave this argument back to God with a simple, "I have already tried Lord, and they said, "No!" Two words resounded within me, "Ask anyway!" I got up off the floor and knew what I had to do. I asked God to give me the right words to say.

The next morning, I went back to the hospital as usual. Around 8:00 am, his team of doctors came into the room. I must pause here and say his team of doctors was the absolute best. The top cardiologist in the hospital had been assigned to his case as they were learning about this disease and how it affected the heart. Although they were there to serve and learn, they also soon found how easy it was to connect with Tom. I knew my chance was standing in front of me. Here I was, an elementary school teacher from the rural mountains, about to propose to a lead team of cardiologists something that they would probably look at me and think to themselves, "You silly woman; do you not think we would have already thought of that if that was even remotely possible?" When I say it took everything inside of me to open my mouth, it is truly an understatement. I silently asked the Lord again to give me the words and opened my mouth.

These words came blundering out of me. "May I ask all of you something?"

"Sure," they answered.

I reminded them of what we had been told when we went to Boston, which was that Tom's heart was too stiff with amyloid to withstand the stem cell transplant. I continued with the question, "What if we were to put Tom on the heart transplant list and get him a new heart? Then he would have a new heart that could withstand a stem cell transplant." Once I started talking, I stayed on a roll. Before they could say anything back, I continued explaining how we knew this would not cure the disease but could give us a few more years together if the stem cell transplant was a success. I reminded them quickly that we had an 8-year-old son at home who needed to have more time with his father. I remember saying, "Imagine the difference that would make in his life if Tom lived five more years to get him to the teenage years." I reminded them that Tom was only 46 and was otherwise healthy if we could slow down this production of amyloid. I know through my voice and eyes, they could see that I was convinced that this could happen only if we could get him on the transplant list.

When I finally stopped my spill, they all just paused and looked at each other. I held my breath as the answer came. Dr. Wells, his lead doctor, stated that she knew he really needed a heart transplant; however, she did not know of any hospital anywhere that would be willing to transplant an amyloid patient, but she would be willing to try to contact several hospitals to see if anyone would be willing to attempt this. The next day she told us that she had called several hospitals across the country, and no one would agree to place him on their list. She said that she was sorry, and she wished she could give us better news and offer some hope. I could tell she desperately wanted to help Tom. I told her that this news came as no surprise as this is what he had been told everywhere we had tried. Several days later, in an attempt to offer Tom one last hope, Dr. Wells asked a hematologist to come by and visit Tom to see if there was any way that he would be willing to attempt a stem cell transplant. She knew that Tom was dying, and they had nothing to lose by trying. After examining him, the hematologist agreed with what we had been told in Boston; his heart would never withstand a stem cell transplant. After telling us this, I was amazed when the hematologist casually stated what I had already voiced to the team of cardiologists, "I know what we need to do, let's get him a new heart and then do the stem cell transplant."

Dr. Wells stated that she had been trying to get hospitals to agree to place him on their list with no luck. Just as simply as his first statement, he replies, "Well, let's do it here!" She was as surprised as we were. We were later told that it had not even entered her mind to do the transplant there. There were two reasons that she had not considered this. One, Baptist Hospital, at that time, had a very small transplant program. They only did about four to six transplants per year. Second, just as we had been told so many times before, hospitals were not willing to put someone on a list with amyloidosis as the chances of it attacking the new organ were probable. Still, here we were hearing someone talk about it. This was our first miracle. For the first time since we discovered his illness, we had a small ray of hope. We had been told before that he had less than a 1% chance of ever getting on a heart transplant list and now someone was at least talking about it. At first, they thought they were out of their mind to even consider putting a man on the list when they knew this could be detrimental to their program if he did not survive. Also, knowing that there were so many people out there in need of a heart, it made more sense to appropriate those hearts to the people who had the best chance of survival.

A couple of days later, we found out that Dr. Wells had been moved off Tom's case and we had a new lead doctor, whose name was Tom as well. He was from South Africa, and I fell in love with his accent. Over the next week, he listened intently to our story from the beginning to the end. He formed a connection to both Tom and me. He asked us questions about our family and our life back in the mountains. My Tom would laugh and joke with him and they soon bonded. The transplant coordinator, Sherry, shared with us that one day after visiting Tom and me, Dr. Wannenburg (Tom) went back to his team of doctors and her, and told all of them that they needed to go up and meet Tom. He told everyone in the meeting, "You are going to like him!" Sherry said her reply was, "I don't want to like him." Sherry stated that she had witnessed so many people die while on the waiting list for an organ over the last year that she just did not even want to know him.

Dr. Wannenburg was persistent that Sherry go up and talk to Tom about transplant and what that involved and start his evaluation. Sherry did come up, and I took this as an optimistic sign, because I knew that she would not be in the room talking with us unless the team was considering putting him on the list. Over the next couple of weeks, several tests were done, medical records were combed through, and the team worked to find out everything they could find on heart transplantation and stem cell transplantation for amyloid. They were only able to find about five patients in the whole world who had undergone cardiac transplantation for amyloidosis. They also confirmed that there was not another center out there that was going to offer any hope, so unless Baptist decided to do the transplant, it would not be done. If larger and more experienced transplant hospitals would not take on his case, then why did this team think they had any chance of success? They continued to ask themselves that very question. Sherry explained that the team did their best to try and talk themselves out of it. The only explanation she offered was that sometimes the circumstances you think are coincidence are the hand of God. Why did Tom end up at their hospital, a very small transplant center that was willing to consider taking a risk of doing it? Sherry said, "We felt this was the right thing for Tom and his family and it was the right thing to do in general. If we and our program went down, I guess we would go down with a bang." The team decided to "bite the bullet" and perform the surgery at their hospital.

It took three weeks of the cardiologist talking to each other, to the head transplant surgeons and then to UNOS, which is the United Network for Organ Sharing, to decide to put him on the list. UNOS is the agency that is contracted by the government to allocate organs. Every transplant center belongs to this organization, and they set policies concerning how organs will be transplanted. Now that the hospital had decided that they would be willing to do the transplant, UNOS's board would need to be convinced as to why this person needed a heart transplant. Tom would also have to be listed as a status 1, which is the highest priority on the list. Paperwork was required to be filled out and sent in to show why there is a situation so critical that the organ is needed. Sherry, who oversaw this paperwork, was concerned that when they found out that Tom had amyloidosis, they would not agree to list him as a status 1 or even deny him being put on their list to receive a heart. They filled out the paperwork, put down the diagnosis and prayed for the best. We were turned down. UNOS did not want to risk giving a heart to an amyloid patient when there were so many others that were in need. All the hope we had built up suddenly went flying back out the window. We had a hospital willing to do the transplant, but now the organization that would provide the organ had become our stopping point, or so we thought.

All hope seemed lost until one morning a couple of days later when Dr. Wannenburg walked into the room. He looked at us with a huge grin on his face and stated, "I have some news!" His expression was not the one of glum and despair that we had become accustomed to seeing on the doctors' faces. Instead, it looked hopeful and happy. I could not imagine, at this point, what he was going to tell us that could change our dismal outlook. He simply stated, "Tom is on the transplant list."

"What?" "How?" These were the exclamations that came blurting out of my mouth. We were flat turned down. What happened to change this? He explained to us that after being turned down, he went back to UNOS and pleaded Tom's case again. Except this time, he didn't just fill out the paperwork and send it as was the protocol. He had found out the names of the members that sat on the board and personally called them. He painted a picture of Tom and his life for them. He told them about his family, his job, and the 8-year-old boy that was waiting on him at home. He said, "I wanted them to know the person behind the request." He said at first, they turned him down again as they had never put an amyloid patient on a transplant list. His reply to them was, "Then you come here to this hospital and meet this man. Talk with him for five minutes, and then see if you can explain to him why he can't be put on the list." He told them to meet his wife who had begged and pleaded for the chance for her husband to receive a new heart so he could have a fighting chance of prolonging his life. He said this seemed to make an impact. After this, they agreed to put him on the list. I broke down crying and praising the Lord at the same time. I then knew why God had kept whispering to me to not give up and to keep asking even after all the rejections we had encountered. I knew that getting a new doctor was not a coincidence. God used him to get to know us and our story and then take that story to go before UNOS one more time and convince them to give him a chance. We knew there was no cure, but even if we could put the disease in remission and have more time together, it would be worth it. We were finally on a transplant list we had been told we had less than a 1% chance of ever being on. I wanted to shout from the rooftop about God's goodness and how he moved a mountain that had such slim odds of being moved.

CHAPTER 6

NEW CHALLENGES

Now that we had finally been put on the list, we had new challenges to face. First, we had to get approval from Tom's insurance to continue to pay for his stay in the Critical Care Unit, approval for the heart transplant as well as the stem cell transplant that would follow if the heart transplant was a success. The doctors had to come up with a plan for how to keep Tom alive while waiting on a donor heart. Waiting for a heart transplant is not like taking a number and waiting your turn. The list is composed of patients with various issues. When a deceased organ donor is identified, UNOS' computer system generates a ranked list of transplant candidates who would be a suitable match to receive that specific organ. UNOS matches individuals waiting for a transplant with a compatible donor organ. There are several factors that come into play when matching donors to recipients. Blood type is crucial to prevent an adverse reaction when the organ is transplanted. The size of the donor organ should be compatible with the recipient's body. Organs are allocated based on urgency. Priority is given to those in critical need. Each patient waiting on the list is listed as a specific status type. Organs must be transported quickly to maintain their viability, so distance becomes a huge factor. Waiting time is another factor. Often priority is given to a patient who has been waiting the longest.

Once again, I went to the Lord in urgent prayer. Tom and I were blessed to be a part of a wonderful church family that had supported us throughout this entire process. Their prayers and support had been a constant for us. I called on them to be in prayer for these specific needs. Our prayer was for approval from our insurance, for a donor heart to become available that had the right body and blood match, for it to be close enough to our hospital to be transported in the time frame and for Tom to be put at the top of the priority list. The most urgent prayer became that God keep Tom alive until a donor heart became available. By this point we had already been in CCU for about three weeks and with every passing day, Tom grew weaker and weaker. Praying for a heart to become available came with mixed emotions. It was hard to pray for a heart for Tom when we knew that would mean that another person would have to lose his/her life. When I prayed, was I asking for someone that matched my husband's blood and body type to die so that he could receive the heart that stopped beating in his/her body? God eased my heart and reminded me that he alone was the giver of life and the ultimate healer. He reminded me that people will die every day and there are those who are selfless and decide while living to become an organ donor. Their act of love was now bringing hope to our situation. For this, Tom and I both were extremely thankful. As soon as I could, I changed my status on my license to become an organ donor so that when I pass, hopefully I could pass this gift along to someone else in need. I had never realized, until it happened to us, the importance of being an organ donor. Organ donation is a way to save a life that otherwise may end needlessly.

    One by one, our prayers were answered. Tom's insurance approved the transplants as well as an extended stay in CCU. Tom was placed on the list as Status 1, which was reserved for the most critically ill and living on the support of a heart-lung bypass machine. Now we would wait and pray that Tom could remain alive until a heart became available.

CHAPTER 7

NOW WE WAIT

School had already started back for me. Thus far, I had been using sick leave to be out and stay at the hospital with Tom. Since we would now be waiting for a heart and there was no way to know how long this may take, I took a leave of absence from work, and they found someone to take my place. I also knew that I would have to leave the hotel as the bills from being there were mounting. I went home for a weekend to see Troy and pack for an extended stay. Brent was away at college, so he was all set. I got everything Troy needed and got him permanently settled at his grandparents. I prayed that God would provide me with a place to stay that wouldn't be as expensive as a hotel. I needed to be close to the hospital. While I was at home, I received a phone call from a coworker that worked at the school where I was a teacher. She informed me that her daughter, Amy, lived in Winston Salem and was a nurse at the same hospital where Tom was a patient. Her daughter lived within ten miles of the hospital and had an extra bedroom at her house. She was calling to offer me the room to stay there as long as needed. Again, God had heard my prayers and sent me a place to stay while I was in Winston Salem. Amy was truly a Godsend during this time for me. Not only did she give me a key to her house and offer for me to come and go as needed, but she was often there to just listen to me cry or pray with me when I would come to her house late at night after spending the day at the hospital.

As we moved into October, it became easy to get discouraged when each day passed and there was no news of a heart. Time became a ticking bomb as I sat and watched the machines that were keeping Tom alive. Through my discouragement, it was always Tom that would lift my spirits and put a smile on my face. He was always ready with a joke, a silly look, or gesture to make me laugh and temporarily take away my worries. I remember one such day when he was scheduled to have a catheterization done in his leg. He asked me to find him a marker. I retrieved one from the nurse's desk not knowing what he could possibly want with a marker. He proceeds to draw an arrow down his leg and writes, "cut here" at the end of the arrow. He wanted the technicians in the Cath Lab to have something to laugh at when they started his procedure. Tom was always thinking of something he could do to put a smile on the doctors, nurses, technicians, or any other person's face that walked into his room. He insisted that I always keep a bowl, on his table, full of candy to give anyone that came in to work with him. If the bowl started to run low, he would instruct me to stop by the store and restock. He would always say, "Make sure you get the good stuff, not the cheap candy that no one wants to eat."

Early in October, even though hooked up to machines, when Tom sat up in the bed or tried to stand up, he would have pre-syncopal episodes, which were times when he would become dizzy and lightheaded and would easily fall and feel as if he would pass out. During the first week in October, he had three such episodes and during one of these he incurred a wound injury that required closure with sutures. It had become apparent that even the slightest movements would cause him to pass out and it was becoming even more dangerous to allow him to try and get up at all. As the month progressed, he developed leukopenia, an abnormally low white blood cell count and was spiking fevers of 103 degrees. Hematology was brought back in and some of his heart medications had to be temporarily decreased to get his white cell count back up.

As we moved into November, we still had no news of a heart. When I say no news, I mean no news of a heart that Sherry felt should be considered. She had received numerous offers from high risks donors who had various diseases from Hepatitis C to AIDS. It was not that she was looking for a heart in pristine condition; however, the heart transplant was only the halfway mark in Tom's journey. He still would have to undergo stem cell transplant, and if he got any other ailments from an infected heart, it would mean the stem cell was out for him. Still, the situation was becoming so desperate that Sherry came in one day and had to ask Tom if he would like her to entertain any of the offers they were getting even though they did not feel it would be in his best interest. He courageously looked at her and said, "No."

On November 12, Tom experienced the first of many episodes where he lost consciousness. He became unresponsive, and the code blue signal started sounding. Doctors and nurses came rushing into the room and began chest compressions and bagging him. I was rushed from the room and went to the restroom next door where I started throwing up and begging God to not let this be the end. We just needed the chance to get him that heart. Please God, do not take him now. Thankfully, they were able to revive him. What had caused him to lose consciousness this time? He had stopped trying to sit or stand up by the bed. Simply, he had tried to roll over in his bed to get some relief from lying on his back. By now, his heart was so weak and damaged with the amyloid that even the movement of rolling over was enough to cause him to pass out. This became the normal pattern over the next couple of weeks. Tom lost consciousness several times and it seemed like with each time, it was getting harder for them to bring him back. I was on constant edge that each time it happened; it would be the last time. I often just stayed at the hospital overnight because he was so close to death and even when I did try to go back to the hotel and sleep, I would often be called back in the middle of the night because he had coded yet again. I knew if that heart did not come soon, it would be entirely too late.

CHAPTER 8

WHEN HEARTACHE CAME KNOCKING AGAIN

On November 20th, his condition was so severe that his doctor only left his side for short periods of time, and his blood pressure was hovering in the 50/30 range. He was 20 pounds overweight with fluid, so they had to place tubes down his throat and nose in an effort to drain it off. I could tell by the look on his doctor's face that he was extremely worried. His condition was so dire that day that I would have called his family to come to the hospital to be by his side; however, that same day his 73-year-old mother had been taken to the emergency room the night before at our local hospital back home. These were the same grandparents Troy was staying with, and they had called my sister to come and take care of him. They had taken Troy out to dinner at a local pizza restaurant and shortly after their return home, she started having severe pain in her chest and esophagus area. She was admitted to the hospital to determine the source of her pain. Overnight, they ran several tests to rule out possible heart and gallbladder issues. These tests came back negative, so a chest x-ray was ordered. Later that afternoon, I called back to the hospital to check on her and was told by a nurse that she had just been put on a helicopter to Baptist hospital; this was the same hospital where we were. After hanging up the phone in total disbelief, Tom's sister called me to tell me they were on their way down and they thought her esophagus had ruptured. I got off the phone and shuffled this information through my mind trying to decide how to let Tom know what his sister had said without upsetting him to the point he would pass out again. I tried to calm my voice and simply told him that she was being sent down where the doctors could take better care of her and reassured him that they didn't think it was an issue with her heart.

Within 45 minutes of hanging up the phone, we saw the helicopter that was carrying Tom's mother go by his window. He looked at me with tears in his eyes and weakly said, "Go to her! Go take care of my mama."

I went down to the emergency room where they had taken her. She was conscious and did not appear to be in too much distress. She was not even sure herself why she had been sent down to Winston. I told her we would get to the bottom of it and figure out what was going on. Shortly after, Dr. Oaks, who was one of the doctors assigned to Tom's case, walked into the room. He was one of the Cardiac Thoracic Surgeons that would be assisting in Tom's heart transplant surgery. My first thought was why is he in here when they did not think it had anything to do with her heart. As soon as he entered the room, he looked at me with the utmost shock on his face. He then looked down at her chart, "Colvard, Colvard, who is this woman to you?" I told him it was Tom's mom and the words, "Oh no!" came pouring out of his mouth. I knew from the look on his face and his tone that something was terribly wrong. By this point they had taken Tom's mom somewhere else, and it was just the two of us in the room. He asked if Tom's dad and sister had arrived yet, and I explained that they were probably still about 30 to 45 minutes away since they were driving. He told me that he needed me to come with him because he had to show me something.

He took me into a room where x-rays were displayed along the wall. It was an obvious chest x-ray, but sprinkled among the chest were little dark blots everywhere. I didn't understand what I was looking at, and then he started to explain. He said that the night before when they had gone out to dinner that she had eaten a salad. Something in the salad, maybe the potato sticks, poked her esophagus and caused it to rupture. When this happened, the food that she was eating spilled out into her chest cavity. Those were the little dark blots that I was seeing. Because the local hospital thought it was her heart, they didn't run a chest x-ray until the next day, so this food had been sitting in her chest cavity for close to 24 hours. When they did run the chest x-ray, they saw what had happened and knew she would need to be immediately transported to a larger hospital. We had come to have a close relationship with Tom's doctors as they came by each day and would spend time talking with us. I could tell that explaining this to me was a strain for him. He said, "I am so sorry this is happening to you as you are already dealing with so much, but I must be honest with you." He explained that her only chance of survival was going immediately into surgery where he would open her up and try the best he could to clean up her chest cavity. You could have literally knocked me over with a feather when he looked at me and said, "She only has about a 25% chance of making it through surgery." I stood there in sheer disbelief. He went on to explain that because the food particles had been in her chest cavity for 24 hours, the chances of major infection were extremely high and if the infection went to her heart, it would kill her. So even if she made it through the surgery, he was not very confident they would be able to stop the infection from spreading to her heart. He asked permission to begin the surgery as they did not have time to wait for her husband and daughter to get there. I gave permission and went back into the room where they were already prepping her. I simply explained to her that she had a small hole in her esophagus, and the doctor was going to go in and repair it. I never told her about the odds the doctor gave me of her survival and assured her we would all be there when she woke up. I prayed over her knowing full well that this may be the last time I saw her alive and these prayers were so very important.

They wheeled her off into surgery, and I went downstairs to the waiting room where I knew that Tom's dad and sister would be coming soon. I sat down on a bench over in the corner and began crying out once again desperately to God. Tom's father had a history of heart issues and had already had several heart attacks in the past. The doctor told him, when Troy was a baby, that his heart was so damaged that he would probably never live to see Troy start school. I asked God for guidance on what to tell him when he walked in the door. This was his wife of 52 years in surgery and his only son was lying upstairs barely hanging onto life. I was so afraid that the shock of it all would cause him to go into cardiac arrest. I remember begging God for help. I was at one of my weakest points.

My mind was imagining the worst of scenarios. How would I explain to my eight-year-old son if the scenario of what could happen to these three people became a reality?

I prayed for guidance on what to go back upstairs and tell Tom. He had sent me downstairs to take care of his mama. Now the only news I had was that she had less than a 25% chance of surviving. I knew that his heart could not take this devastating news. In a few minutes, Tom's father and sister walked through the door. His father's face was white, and I could tell by his gait that he was weak and worried. I knew I had to tell them what was happening and explain about her being taken into surgery. I told them the details leaving out the part about the 25% chance of survival. That was the one detail that I was afraid would cause him the most stress. In a few moments, he went to the restroom, and I told Tom's sister just how serious this was and the bleak facts the doctor had quoted me. I told her she would have to make the decision of how much she thought her father could handle knowing. She agreed with me that we would not tell him how serious it was and pray for a better outcome. I was holding onto faith that she would pull through the surgery and the infection would be contained, and he would never have to know just how close he was to losing her at that moment.

After speaking with them, I went back upstairs to Tom's room. He was anxious to hear news of his mother. I decided to tell him, just as I had his father, only the details that he had to know. I explained that she was in great hands with Dr. Oaks. That made Tom feel better, knowing that she was with one of the top surgeons in the hospital, and he had confidence that he would take good care of her. After a few hours, we got word that she had made it through surgery and would now be taken to ICU where she would be placed on high-powered antibiotics to try and prevent infection. God had pulled her through the surgery; we needed now to pray her through recovery. Meanwhile, as this was going on with his mother, Tom continued to grow weaker and had even more episodes of losing consciousness and having to be revived. With all of this going on, I basically had just started staying at the hospital around the clock. As I stated before, one of my worst fears was that he would pass away, and I would not be there. When I did leave the hospital, I went back to the hotel that was beside the hospital so I could be there quickly if needed. Although

I was still welcome to stay at Amy's house, things had gotten too critical for me to feel like I wanted to drive those 10 miles from her house to the hospital. Most nights, even if I did go to the hotel, I would get the call to come back, because he had coded again. There was never any peace, any rest and that time bomb that kept ticking was about to go off. Tom was holding on by a thread, his mother was still in the hospital fighting infection, and I was totally at the end of my rope.

CHAPTER 9

WHEN GOD SHOWED UP IN A MIGHTY WAY

It was Monday night, November 25th, and I had just left the hospital around 10:00 pm. It had been the usual day of watching the machines and praying that Tom make it through one more day. By this point, Tom had been in the hospital for a total of 86 days. The only break in these days was the five days that we were able to go home at the end of August. I was emotionally and physically drained. I had been juggling responsibilities both at the hospital and home. I had only been back home a few times over these 86 days to see Troy and catch up quickly on bills. Continuing to watch Tom decline and the emotional weight of the situation was taking a toll on me. The feelings of helplessness and hopelessness grew stronger with each passing day. There was better news concerning his mother. It seemed that she was beating the odds and fighting off the infection. The doctors were amazed and impressed with her recovery, and they declared it a miracle that she was even alive. I decided to go to the hotel and try to rest and get a shower with plans to be back the next morning. I walked into the parking deck at Baptist hospital to try and find my car. I literally stopped in the middle of one of the levels, not even sure where I had parked. I was so tired, so broken, and so drained. I didn't have anything left in me any longer. I fell on my knees right there in the parking lot and started crying so hard. I told God I cannot do this anymore. I had been fighting for

Tom for over a year now, and we did not seem to be any closer to getting a heart than we were three months ago. God had been my source of strength through it all, but I guess I was just so exhausted from everything, I just crashed. I begged him to give me a sign he was still there, and a heart was coming. I was honest with God and told him that my faith was weak, and I was tired. At that point, I didn't think my heart could hold any more pain and I didn't know how to continue the fight. I told him that he would have to pick me up and give me something to keep me going.

I finally got up, found my car and went to the hotel. I fell into bed from exhaustion, and this ended up being one night that I didn't have to return to the hospital. I awoke the next morning and was thankful for the rest. When I got up out of bed, I quickly noticed that I had started my period during the night. My first thought was just great; what else can go wrong? I wasn't prepared as everything was off in my body from all the stress it was under. I got up to jump in the shower and prepare to go to the hospital. I quickly noticed that blood had leaked into the bed on the sheets. I stood there staring down at this stain that had been made and could not believe what I was seeing. Looking down at this white sheet, I saw a perfectly formed symmetrical heart where I had just been lying. This heart could not have been more perfect if I had taken a red marker and drawn it there myself. I remembered the night before when I had prayed for God to give me a sign so that my strength would be renewed, and I could continue this fight. I immediately knew that God had sent me that sign that I had prayed for so desperately. I stood there and cried once more, except these tears were tears of thankfulness and praise to God for answered prayer. His symbol gave me the strength to continue the fight. I raced through the shower with renewed energy and could not wait to get to the hospital to tell Tom what had happened.

I rushed into Tom's room and said, "You are never going to believe what happened?" I went through all the details of the night before and how I had cried out to God. I then told him about the blood stain and how it had formed a perfect heart. He looked at me with that big grin that always warmed my heart. He then stated, "Well, God wanted you to have a double sign." I looked at him in confusion and asked what he meant. During the night, Tom had a bleed in the port-a-cath in his neck. They had to take it out and replace it with a new one. Tom turned his neck to show me where the bleeding had happened. At once, I saw what he was talking about. Where his catheter bled out, the blood had formed a perfectly symmetrical heart underneath his skin. The heart was literally the exact same size as the heart that had been in my bed earlier. God not only had sent us one sign, but two. We looked at each other and knew that God was sending us a loud message that he was there and still holding us in his arms. There was not a doubt in my mind that God was about to show up in a mighty way.

Within thirty minutes of my arrival at the hospital, Sherry, our Heart Transplant Coordinator, walked into our room, looked at us with a big smile, and said, "We've got a heart!"

CHAPTER 10

THE TRANSPLANT

"We've got a heart!" The words we had been waiting to hear for months were finally being spoken. Sherry then goes on to tell us that a man close to Tom's age and size with a matching blood type had been in a fatal accident in Georgia. The man was an organ donor. She said that they were flying down to look at the heart. If it looked as good as it did on the paper they received, then they would be back with a new heart for Tom. We all stood there momentarily crying, laughing and hugging each other. God had answered our prayers; this and the two heart signs we received earlier made three hearts we received that morning. Sherry and her team did not have a lot of time to stand around and talk at this point. A donor heart can only remain viable for transplant for around four to six hours. Sherry and the team left, and we quickly started making phone calls. As stated before, Tom and I were blessed with an amazing church family, friends and family that had continually rallied around us throughout this entire process. Our pastor had been so faithful to come and visit us several times every week since we had entered the hospital. As fate would have it, he had walked into the room that morning just before Sherry came in with her announcement of having a possible heart. He had been such a part of our journey, and Tom and I were both glad he was there with us when we received this news. Our pastor and I started calling people back home to start a prayer chain that this heart would be acceptable, and the team would make it back in time to transplant. Within a couple of hours, we had a waiting room full of family and friends that had arrived at the hospital to be there with us. Also, a team of church members had gathered at our church to pray. With these prayers going up for Tom and this heart, we felt a peace and joy that only God could give.

Soon, we got the news we had been waiting to hear. The heart, upon inspection, was found to have no defects or injury from the donor's accident. They were on the way back to the hospital with the heart. The transplant team started working with Tom to get him ready and everything started moving very quickly. He would need to be prepped and ready when the heart arrived. Surgeons would need to be ready to work swiftly to ensure the heart's viability. They came to get Tom to take him down to the operating room to get him prepared. As previously stated, Tom could not even roll over in the bed at this point without passing out and his condition was beyond critical. When the team lifted him up from his bed to put him on the gurney to take him downstairs for surgery, he passed out. Once again, I was standing there praying, Lord please let him come back. We have a heart almost here; we made it. He can't die now! Thankfully, the team was able to revive him, but everyone knew this heart couldn't get here fast enough. I gave Tom a kiss and told him that we would see him in a few hours and with that new heart he would be able to get up and do a dance. We all went downstairs to the waiting room and held hands forming a large circle. By this time, there were around 25 people there waiting with us. As our pastor led us all in prayer for a successful surgery, I could feel the love and support of everyone there as well as back home. We knew that we had armies of people praying for Tom. Our church family, my workplace, Tom's workplace, and just our small-town community in general. That was one blessing of being from a small town. Everyone knew Tom and his situation, and he probably was on every prayer list in our county. News had spread across our small town that morning that he had finally received a heart and prayers were going up everywhere. I have never felt so covered in prayer in my life. It was not long before I received a call from Sherry that they were beginning the surgery, and she would keep me updated as they progressed through it. Relief washed over me that Tom had stayed alive until they could get a heart and get him on the operating table. Every minute had been so critical up to that point, and there were so many times that we almost lost him. I felt like I could breathe for the first time in months. Once again, the quote that he had less than a 1% chance of getting on a heart transplant list entered my mind. Not only did God put him on the list, but now he was giving him a new heart. Thankfulness flooded my soul.

During a heart transplant, the old heart is taken out and the new heart is sewn in its place. A heart-lung bypass machine continues to pump blood throughout the body during this process. The surgeon then connects blood vessels and once the new heart is securely in place, the tubes from the bypass machine are removed. Blood circulation is then directed back into the new heart. Electrical shocks are administered to stimulate the heart and as it warms up, it begins beating on its own. Once it starts beating on its own, then the patient is removed from the heart-lung bypass machine, and the new heart takes over from there. Sherry told us later that she asked the surgeons before they started, "What happens if the heart doesn't start beating on its own?" In the past, Sherry had been a coordinator for kidney transplants and was not accustomed to being in the operating room for a heart transplant. The surgeon's reply to her was, "Oh Sherry, think about infection or bleeding or something, but don't think about that; it always beats."

We had been in the waiting room for some time when Sherry called me back with an update. I picked up the phone anxiously waiting for the good news I was about to receive. Instead, Sherry, with a concerned tone, states, "Sandra, it is not going well up here. We have the heart sewn in and it is not beating. Usually, a heart will beat in the first five minutes, and we have been working with it for about ten minutes, and it just won't beat." She said she just wanted to let me know what was going on and they would keep working. I got off the phone and we quickly got everyone back in a circle to pray and my friend called back to our church to have everyone there to turn up the heat on those prayers going up. I felt panic once again rise up in my soul, but at the same time, I had faith that God would not bring us this far to just lose him on the operating table. In another five to ten minutes, Sherry called me back to say, "Sandra, it is still not beating, and you need to pray, I mean pray really hard, and we are going to pray up here over him as well." I could hear in her voice that she thought all hope was lost. I now know that she knew it was not working, and she was thinking

MIRACLE OF THE HEARTBEAT

how she was going to come down and tell us that they had lost him on the operating table. I now know that if a heart doesn't start beating in the first 15-20 minutes, then there is very little chance of it beating at all. We were now past the 20-minute mark. Normally when you shock a heart, you can see the little squiggly line come up on the heart monitor. They had been continually shocking it for 20 minutes, and it did nothing but flatline. It had not made as much as a flutter on the screen. I got off the phone once again and relayed the news to everyone standing in the room. Our pastor states, "Well, we just keep praying. God is not finished with Tom yet." We prayed and everyone back home was praying. In a few minutes, my phone rang again. Once again, it was Sherry. I braced myself. I would love to say that I had faith that she was calling to deliver good news, but my wife's heart was sinking and preparing for the worst. Through tears and shouts, Sherry exclaims, "It's beating! The heart started beating!" The impossible had happened, and the heart was finally beating in Tom's chest. She said she would be down later to talk with us and share the miracle that had happened in the room.

When Sherry came down, she explained that they were ready to give up. She said that no matter how many times they shocked it, it just was not beating. She was preparing herself, as it was her job, to come down and tell us that Tom did not make it off the operating table. She said the surgeons paced the room not wanting to give up. As I said before, Tom had become like family to everyone at the hospital. We had been there so long, and they all desperately wanted to save him. In addition, they had taken a huge risk by agreeing to perform this surgery at their hospital. A risk no other hospital was willing to take. Not only for Tom, but for the sake of their program, they needed this surgery to be a success. One of the surgeons told the other that they needed to call it because it just was not working. They all walked away from the table, feeling defeated and dreading having to deliver us the blow they knew it would be. Suddenly, when they all walked away, the new heart started beating on its own. Sherry went on to tell us, when it started beating, it was not one of those little lines you might see on the screen, but a perfect line with a perfect rhythm. She said that everyone in the room just paused and looked at each other in utter disbelief. One of the surgeons stated that it must have been God that started that heart, because they sure could not get it to start.

Not only did God start Tom's heart, but he was able to come out of the operating room with less IV drips than what is normally given to someone who had been transplanted. After surgery, Tom was taken to the Intensive Care Unit and listed in stable condition. Stable was a word that we had not heard used to describe Tom's condition since finding out about this disease. Just hearing the word stable brought peace and comfort to my heart. By day one post-op, the flow of blood within the organs and tissues of his body was rated as satisfactory, and by day two, he was weaned from any ventilatory support and extubated to a 40% face shield. By day three, he was successfully weaned from all drips that he had been using since surgery and the next day all his drains were discontinued. These drains had been used to remove unwanted fluids that build up in the body. On day five, after Tom's surgery, he was able to be moved out of Intensive Care to a post-surgical unit. For the first time in 91 days, we were in a regular room instead of a Critical/Intensive Care Unit.

Over the next couple of days, Tom was able to tolerate a regular diet and even started getting up and walking down the hallways. Once he was allowed to get out of bed and move outside of his room, there was one place he wanted to go. As soon as they would allow him to do so, Tom wanted to go see his mama. She was still in the hospital recovering from her surgery. Against all odds, she survived the surgery and fought the infection. Since Tom was critical when she came in and then went into surgery shortly thereafter, he had not been able to see her. Likewise, she was confined to Intensive Care during Tom's surgery and could not be there with the rest of the family. She was now in a regular room, and Tom was cleared to see her. The nurse rolled him down to her room in a wheelchair, and the reunion that took place was an image I will never forget. Tom burst into tears seeing the mother that he didn't think he would ever see again. She was overcome with emotion as the son that she had prayed for and knew was critical for months was now in the room beside her. They hugged and cried and there was not a dry eye in the room including the doctors and nurses that were in there with us. As a family we had so much to be thankful for. Tom's mother had survived and would be going home soon, and Tom had his new heart. For the first time in over a year, our world didn't look bleak, but promising and full of hope.

CHAPTER 11

GOING HOME

On December 6, after being in a hospital for 96 days, we were given the best Christmas present imaginable. We were cleared to go home. We left with extensive instructions on medication, diet, activity levels and wound care. The heart transplant was only half of Tom's journey. Now to get him strong enough so that he could undergo the stem cell transplant. Going home, together, seemed like a dream come true. There were so many times that I did not think we would ever be back in our home as a family. I longed for the simple things in life that can so easily be taken for granted. I couldn't wait to just be home and cook dinner, do laundry and get Troy ready for school. We knew that activity would be limited, and we would be basically confined to the house until we could get through the stem cell transplant, but it didn't matter. We would be home and be together. Our goal was to settle in and just enjoy being a family while Tom grew in strength to be ready to face the next battle. In addition, it was the Christmas season, and I couldn't wait to get home and put up a tree and decorate. I was looking forward to having some normalcy back in our lives again. As happy as I was, I know it was only a small fraction of the elation that Tom was feeling. I remember going to get the car, when they discharged him, and driving around to the pick-up door. They wheeled Tom out and the look on his face when he breathed the fresh air and looked up at the blue sky was a sight to behold. I imagine that after lying on his back for months, staring at death's door, and then being able to see all of God's beauty again was overwhelming.

As we drove the hour and a half ride home, he sat and just looked out the window. He seemed to be noticing everything. Again, all the little things that one takes for granted daily suddenly become the big things that mean so much. He was so humble, thankful and feeling so very blessed. Soon we had made the climb up highway 16 to the top of the mountain. As we came around a curve just as we were entering Ashe County, we looked up and before us was a huge billboard. On this billboard, a banner had been put up with the words, "WELCOME HOME TOM!" After many months of being gone, Tom was being welcomed back into our small town and the love of the people was shining through on this billboard. Tom broke down in tears and again was so very humbled by the love and support from all our family and friends. As shocking as this was to both of us, it paled in comparison to what was waiting on us as we turned into our driveway. When we arrived home, our driveway, yard, and porch were filled with people cheering for us. People had come from Tom's work, my school, our church and community to welcome us home. Signs, balloons and banners were everywhere to show Tom how loved he was and how thankful people were to have him come back home. We got out of the car, and Tom stood there and just cried. People were very respectful not to come up and touch or hug him as they knew he would be immunocompromised for a while. However, the love and support they gave us as they rallied around us was a true testament to what community is all about and people showing the love of Christ. Just when we did not think we could be any more surprised, we went inside the house. Our house had been cleaned from top to bottom, our refrigerator and pantry stocked with food and our dining room floor was lined with basics such as paper towels, laundry detergent, toilet paper, etc. A Christmas tree stood proudly in our living room, ready for us to decorate. Our friends and family had truly thought of everything. Working together, our community of support had created an environment where the only thing we would have to think about when we returned home was getting Tom better. Once again, gratitude flooded both of our souls.

We began getting Tom settled in, and thanks to everyone's generosity, I did not need to worry about going to the grocery store or to do food prep, as our friends also set up a meal train to deliver meals for some time. This allowed me to focus on the list of instructions from Tom's doctors. Tom was put on ten different medications, and several of these had to be taken three to four times per day. I had to come up with a system to organize his medicine to ensure he was taking them in the right dosage and at the proper times. We also had to record his temperature, pulse, and weight daily. Every day started with a thorough inspection of his wounds, from surgery, to ensure there was no redness or drainage. Tom was growing stronger every day, and it was such a miracle to see him up and walking about the house. I had never been so happy to just be home and do the everyday mundane things that need to be done to keep a home running.

We were fast approaching Christmas, and we all knew that we would be looking at the season through a different lens than ever before. Christmas breakfast is a tradition that my oldest sister started when I was seven years old. When the families of my two brothers and two sisters, along with mine, get together, it creates quite a houseful of love and togetherness. This Christmas was going to be just a little bit more special than any in the past. My niece had brought the family together, prior to Christmas, and created a surprise video that was played for Tom this Christmas morning. Each person in my family had recorded a message for Tom letting him know how thankful they were that he was home and shared a special memory of him. The video also showed a timeline of Tom's life, our marriage and family, and major events in our lives. Everyone arrived at my sister's house, had our breakfast, opened our gifts and then everyone settled in to watch the video with Tom. There were so many tears and so much laughter as we reminisced through the journey that was Tom's life --- Tom's life, a life that was still here; a life that had survived so much over the past year. Tears of gratitude, thankfulness and just humility ran down Tom's face as he watched the love pour out of others for him. He was with us for Christmas, and since there were too many times that we were not sure this holiday would be spent with him; we all knew what a miracle it was that we were sharing this Christmas morning.

Tom was still not able to go out to the store or be around a lot of people. If he continued to heal and recover as planned, he would be able to have his stem cell transplant in April. We had to make sure that he stayed well and grew stronger to withstand this next step of our journey. Although he knew this was necessary, it bothered him that he would not be able to go out and buy me a Christmas present. I assured him that I did not need another gift as I felt I had truly been given the best present ever by him just coming back home and us being a family again. So, imagine my surprise when on Christmas day, he handed me a beautifully wrapped package. I looked at him in surprise with eyes I'm sure were asking, "How did you get this?" Before I could ask him, he told me that there was something that he wanted me to have that once meant a lot to me, but I lost it. He wanted to make sure that it was replaced. He had a coworker go all over our town and a neighboring town until she could find this for him. I opened the gift, with absolutely no idea what he was talking about; replacing something I lost? Early in our marriage, I had told Tom about a Raggedy Ann doll that I had when I was a little girl. We did not have a lot of toys when we were growing up, but this doll was one treasure I had, and she was my best friend. I slept with her every night and often shared conversations with her that no one else heard. She was my comfort when I was lonely and just needed someone to hug. When I went away to college, Raggedy Ann went with me. Somewhere during those college years, Raggedy went missing and although I looked everywhere for her, she was never found. I was heartbroken and truly felt like I had lost a family member. I opened this gift, that Tom had put so much effort into getting for me and could not believe my eyes. In the box was a Raggedy Ann doll. A beautiful Raggedy Ann doll that was a close replica of the one I had when I was a little girl. Sewn on her dress was a wooden heart. Tears began streaming down my face as I knew the reason he wanted me to have this doll. My thoughts were confirmed when he looked at me and said, "One day when I'm gone, I want you to remember how much comfort she gave you as a child and let her be a source of comfort for you again. When you hug her, remember how much you are loved and treasured." I am sure that this gesture may seem silly to some people, but to me it was the best physical gift I had ever received. I knew the love and reason behind it. I found out later from the coworker who helped him that he insisted she keep looking everywhere until she found one. This was long before Amazon started selling products other than books. It was important to him for me to have this doll, as he knew, even then, that his time would be limited with us.

 Over the next couple of months, Tom was constantly taking care of "matters" that were important to him. Even though he was getting stronger, and everything seemed to be progressing as expected, we still did not know if the stem cell transplant would be successful and put the disease into remission. We were optimistic about the future, but I also knew there were things that Tom wanted to make sure he took care of in the event things did not go as planned. One of these things was to get Troy a puppy. Tom had grown up in a house where they always kept a schnauzer dog. He often talked about his dogs he had as a child, and he wanted Troy to have the same experience that he had. So, one weekend, he took him to purchase a schnauzer puppy. They came home with a little pup, which Troy named Heidi. Heidi quickly became part of our family and was Troy's constant companion until she passed away when Troy was a freshman in college. Another thing Tom wanted to do was to get Brent a vehicle. When Brent was 16, we had purchased him a reliable, but used, car for his birthday. We did not believe in giving a 16-year-old a new vehicle as we felt they needed time to learn and allow for possible mishaps. By this point, Brent was finishing up his second year in college. He had been driving the same used car since he was 16, and Tom felt it was time for an upgrade. He wanted to be the one to give it to him. Brent's dream car was a Chevy Trailblazer. Tom worked with our local dealership to have one delivered and hid it in our garage. Brent came home one weekend from college to visit. When he arrived at the house on Friday night, Tom soon found an excuse to send him out to the garage. Brent opened the door, with us sneakily trailing behind him, to find his new vehicle sitting there. Tom told him that he knew his old car was getting a lot of mileage on it and now he wouldn't have to worry about those drives back and forth to Chapel Hill.

Before Tom got sick, he was a huge fan of all things Nascar. He enjoyed attending as many races as possible and had started a small collection of memorabilia. Since he would be spending so much time isolated before the stem cell transplant in April, we decided to take his love of the sport and expand it indoors as much as possible. We had a room above our garage that had been partially finished. We decided to complete this room and turn it into Tom's personal "Nascar Room." Tom decorated the room with all things racing. He put his favorite driver's posters on the walls, had his model cars lined up around the room and even had a Nascar lamp installed. He loved this room and spending time in it gave him great joy.

There were still many days Tom did not feel well as he was still battling with the pain that the amyloidosis continually brought to his nervous system. Although he had a new heart, the disease was still attacking his nervous system and would be until hopefully the stem cell transplant put it in remission and eased his symptoms. Having this room to focus on, over the next couple of months, made the days not seem so long for him. The best part of his day always came around 3:00 pm when Troy came home from school, and he would get to spend that time with him.

Traveling back to Baptist Hospital every other week became part of our normal routine as Tom had to have follow up heart biopsies to monitor for possible rejection. After a heart transplant, the body may perceive the donor heart as a foreign object and start an immune response against it. This is known as heart transplant rejection. Although rejection is most common in the first several weeks after transplantation, it can happen months, or even years after the surgery, despite the use of immunosuppressant drugs. These regular biopsies would help detect possible rejection even if there were no symptoms.

CHAPTER 12

STEM CELL TRANSPLANT

Finally, we made it to April. So far, everything had gone well with Tom. Some of his biopsies had shown some minor symptoms of rejection, but we would stay in the hospital for a couple of days to get treatment and get back on track. Most importantly, the biopsies showed no amyloid deposits had formed on his new heart. Even though we were facing another stay in the hospital and another transplant, we were very optimistic that we were well on our way to putting this disease into remission and with Tom's new heart, he would have many years yet to live. With a successful stem cell transplant, many amyloid patients go on to live an average of 15 years with some patients surviving greater than 20 years. This was a much better statistic than we had been quoted just a year before when we were facing three to six months. We checked back into the hospital on April 9 and were told to plan on being there for five to six weeks. Once admitted, Tom's healthy stem cells were harvested from his blood, and he started receiving melphalan-based chemotherapy twice per day. As stated earlier, amyloidosis occurs when white blood cells do not function properly. These cells generate abnormal proteins that misfold into amyloid fibrils and then deposit in various organs of the body. Once a patient's own stem cells are collected from their blood and stored temporarily, chemotherapy is administered to destroy these abnormal cells. After chemotherapy, the stored stem cells are returned to the patient's body via a vein. Once these cells are infused back into the body, they will grow and mature into new blood cells, replacing the cells that were killed during treatment. Tom was given chemotherapy for five days before the transfusion was done on April 14. During these five days he developed mucositis (an inflammation of the mouth and GI tract). He also ran a fever which thankfully responded to antibiotics.

The first five days of this new hospital stay turned out to be very rough on him, but even as poorly as he felt, there was something weighing heavy on his heart. It just so happened that my 40th birthday was on April 11, just two days after we had checked into the hospital. When we first received the schedule for the stem cell transplant, Tom's first remark was that it was my birthday, and he didn't want us to be in the hospital during it. He wanted to see if they could postpone it for another week. I would have no part of that and insisted that we go ahead as scheduled. My birthday was not even a factor to be considered as the quicker we got through the transplant, the quicker we put this disease in remission. So, on April 11, when I walked into his hospital room, he handed me what appeared to be a stack of brown napkins. He looked up at me and said apologetically, "I was not able to go out to a store to buy you a birthday card, so I made do with what I had." While I had gone to the hotel overnight, and in his sickly state, he had written me a birthday card/letter on the stack of napkins that were on his food tray. I was so deeply touched by this selfless gesture. Here he was in a hospital bed feeling the effects from the high dose chemotherapy, but still he found the strength to write these words to me.

Sandra —

Where should I begin to tell you how much your truly loved on this day! Your 40th birthday!

I am so thankful to have been able to share your last 18 birthdays — Today, I am "really", "really" glad to be here to share this day — !!

I'm so sorry that your birthday had to fall at a time during which I'm in the hospital — It's not fair to you; but soon, I will be able to make it up to you — I have some plans for "you" .... later.

Tonight, as I lay here in this hospital bed, I can only

think about how truly unselfish a person you really are. You have stuck with me and loved me like no one else could. The last year has been in such disarray, that I don't see how you've managed our home with such fortitude and willingness to keep us "afloat" during a time in which most wives would have collapsed-

God has blessed you with an inner "spunk" that only could have came from your Dad's side of the family. You not only play "Mom" 24/7, but take care of me, yourself, Heidi and our home with giving 100% of your time to others— You're a special lady... one which I have been with, and want to share another 40 years with! I Love you, Happy Birthday Mama, Mama Jo, Dumpling Cakes, Sweet Pea, and many more! I know it won't be the same, but we're gonna celebrate when we get home. Us'ins has got plans fer yeah! Ha! Ha, 40 40 Hee Haw, + Love you! Tom

This was yet another example of Tom's resilience and strength. No matter what he was going through, or had been through, I never once heard him complain about his situation, pain or possible outcome with this disease. He always spent his time thinking of others, especially his family. He constantly worried about me and the toll that his illness had taken on my health and well-being. He did not realize that my strength came from watching him be so incredibly strong and brave. Needless to say, I still have these napkins with my birthday wishes written on them and I will forever be grateful for this unique treasure that was my 40th birthday gift.

CHAPTER 13

GOING HOME, AGAIN

T om continued to do so well that we were able to go home on April 27th. What was supposed to be a five-to-six-week hospital stay turned out to be less than three weeks. We had two transplants behind us and a future to get back home to begin. A future that for over a year did not seem possible based on any human reasoning or explanation. However, as Isaiah 41:10 tells us, "I will hold you up with my victorious right hand." God had answered our prayers, moved mountains and been by our side holding us up with his enduring love and support.

Troy was out of school shortly after we returned home from the transplant. We wanted to make summer plans and enjoy living again. We knew that his little life had been turned upside down and we wanted to make it a fun and special summer. Also, due to the need for Tom to stay healthy for the stem cell transplant, he had not been allowed to be out of the house much. He was excited to be able to get out and see people and just participate in life again. We still had the daily round of medicines to administer and monitor his vitals for heart rejection, but he was finally cleared to be around people and go in public places.

Tom's 47th birthday was on June 5th, and I wanted to make sure this was an extra special event for him. I gathered up family and friends to help me plan a surprise birthday party. The fact that he was with us here on this birthday was so much to celebrate. Also, we had had so much support from family and friends, over the past year, that I knew it would be special for

Tom to have them all in one place where he could personally thank them and let them know just how much their support and prayers had meant to him. With a lot of behind-the-scenes planning, we had it all arranged. Our families and friends would be at our church fellowship hall and be ready to surprise him when we arrived. Two of our best friends and I told him that we were taking him out for dinner for his birthday. Suddenly, one of the friends remembered that he needed to stop by the church to get something he supposedly left there, as we were on our way to the restaurant. When we pulled up in the church parking lot, around 200 people came out to surprise him with a loud "Happy Birthday!" He was in total shock, and I was so happy that we had pulled off the surprise without him even being suspicious that something was happening other than a dinner out with friends. Tom stood in the fellowship hall and cried humble tears as he thanked everyone that came out and for all the love and support they had given him. I think everyone else in the room cried as well. A journal had been purchased and each family that was represented had written a special message in it for Tom. When we returned home that night, he sat down and read every word in his new journal and we both were in awe at the goodness of God and the love of people in our lives.

Tom had always been a lover of the beach. This was one of the first things he wanted us to do together. One of our friends that came to his birthday party knew that Tom loved the beach. At his party, he told Tom that we were welcome to use his grounded camper that stayed at Ocean Lakes Campground in Myrtle Beach anytime we wanted to use it. We had never stayed at a campground at the beach but thought this might be a good thing to do since it wouldn't be as crowded as a hotel and would give us a little more privacy. We took him up on his offer and planned our trip the same week that we knew some other friends would be going. This was a first-time experience for both Tom and me. We were not sure how we would like staying in a camper or in a campground for that matter. We had always lodged in hotels in the past when we went to the beach. We were both surprised with how quickly we fell in love with the whole camping experience. Being in a campground was more laid back and more enjoyable than being in a hotel. Troy and his friends were able to ride around in a golf cart and explore. We all spent our days around the pool or down on the beach and our nights gathered around campfires roasting marshmallows. By the end of the week, we were all hooked. When we got back home, we decided that we liked it so much that we wanted to purchase our own camper. This would be the perfect way to enjoy our summer and allow Troy to spend time with other kids as so many of our friends had campers. We went camper shopping and were fortunate to find the perfect fifth wheel camper that would serve us well. We took many other camping trips over the summer with friends to local campgrounds in our area. These trips were a bonding time for us as a family and we were able to make many wonderful memories together.

Another thing that was important for Tom to do was to give his testimony at our church. Our pastor had told him earlier that when he felt the time was right that he would like for him to share our story with the church. Tom knew the time was right and set it up to speak on July 13th. Tom, Troy and I all spoke during this service outlining different parts of the past year and a half. There was no way to tell everything that had happened over this period so we chose the events in which we felt would give God the most glory. We were also fortunate that Sherry drove up from Winston to be a part of our service as well. She was able to give a firsthand account of what had happened in the operating room the day of the heart transplant. During Tom's part of the service, he described how he would talk to God, as he lay in the hospital, and ask him to surround him with his peace and love. He stated there was not a day or night that went by that he couldn't feel God with him and surrounding him with a peace that words just can't explain. He felt like God's angels were taking care of him every way that he turned. At the end of the service, Tom and our pastor explained how everyone could find this peace that only comes from knowing our Father. The altar was lined with people that day that gave their hearts to Christ. After the service, Tom looked at me and said, "That just made everything I went through worth it. If even one person would have come to the altar, it would have been worth it!"

CHAPTER 14

WHEN AUGUST CAME

As we moved into August, we reflected on how our summer had been everything that we hoped it would be. We enjoyed beach trips, camping trips and time with our families and friends. However, the best part of the summer for me was just us all being home together and doing the normal everyday aspects of life. It is so easy to take the chores of life for granted or even dread having to complete them. When you are not able to just wake up and go to your job, when you are not able to be in your home cooking dinner, doing laundry, or tucking your child in at night, your perspective changes. I realized that all these little mundane moments that we trudge through daily are really what make up most of life and make it worth living. On one specific day, I was standing at my kitchen sink cleaning up after dinner. Tom and Troy had gone outside to wash off the car. Troy had pulled his "toy vehicles" to the pavement and was washing them off as well. I watched through the window as they started spraying each other with the water hose and chasing each other around the yard. Two very distinct thoughts went through my mind as I watched this scene play out in front of me. One, I had never felt happier in my life. This was living, and I was so thankful to the Lord for giving us these precious moments that just a year ago seemed impossible. My next thought, "Lord, please put this disease in remission so that Troy can continue to have many more water fights with his father."

Since it was August, Troy would be going back to school. I was also going back to my job of teaching. Tom was now able to stay at home on his own, and I looked forward to getting back to my students. Tom had been put on long-term disability, and it was not clear at this point when or if he would be cleared to go back to his job. It was the first week of August, and we were getting everything prepared for Troy and me to start back to school. I noticed that Tom seemed to have less energy than usual. We had learned that when this happens, it may mean his heart is showing signs of rejection. So as usual, we called Sherry and described his symptoms. She told us to bring him down, and Tom was admitted on August 6th to rule out transplant rejection. He spent the night going through the usual tests and was sent home the next day with his labs showing no signs of rejection.

With Troy and I back in school, Tom willingly took over the chores around the house. He would have dinner ready when we came home and delighted in being able to take care of us. Over the next couple of weeks, we settled into a routine. Life was good and we were happy. We had planned our next camping trip with our friends to go to Pigeon Forge and take the kids to Dollywood. Our trip was set for August 22-24th and we all looked forward to it. During the week we were to leave for the trip, I noticed that Tom's energy level seemed to once again be low. I questioned him about it and told him that he needed to rest more during the day and not try to do as much around the house. Friday came and Tom really did not feel well. We were due to leave for the trip, and I told him that I didn't think we should go. He was adamant that we were going. He did not want to disappoint Troy, and he was looking forward to getting away as well. I told him to at least call Sherry and let her know what was going on. He called her and let her know his symptoms and told her about the weekend trip. Since he had just had a clear heart biopsy on August 6th, she told him that she thought he would be fine but made him promise to come to the hospital first thing on Monday morning, upon our return, and get checked out. He promised he would be there on Monday, and we left for our trip.

We set up our camper alongside the other families who had joined us at the campground. Troy and all the other children played, went swimming and rode their bikes. On Saturday, all the families went to Dollywood together. Troy wanted to go on a ride that you had to walk up a hill to access. He told his daddy, "Come, ride this with me!" I remember the look on Tom's face being one of apprehension when Troy asked him. Regretfully, Tom said to him that he did not think he had the energy to walk up that hill. One of our friends quickly picked up on this and said to Troy, "I'll go ride it with you." This greatly concerned me. This was the first time, since recovering from the heart transplant, I had heard Tom say anything like this. I asked him what was wrong. He brushed it off and just said that he was feeling a little winded and didn't think he could walk up that hill. The thought raced through my head again that we shouldn't have come on this trip and gone ahead to the hospital. I even tried to get him to consider leaving and going back that day instead of waiting one more day. He assured me that he was fine, and he was not going back any earlier than planned. He reminded me that he would get it checked out on Monday. We all went back to our campers, and Tom and Troy decided to go for a swim. I was preparing our dinner to be grilled when they came back. Tom relayed to me that he and Troy were the only two in the pool. He said it was so nice to have that time for just the two of them. The next morning, we all awoke and prepared to start packing up our campers to return home. Everyone planned to go to the Apple Barn for breakfast before we left. When I came out of the camper, I saw Tom sitting at the picnic table staring off into space. I asked him if he was ready to go for breakfast and he said that he wasn't hungry and was just going to stay there and finish packing up the camper. He said for me and Troy to go ahead with the others, and he would be ready to leave when we returned. Again, this concerned me, as this was not like Tom to not want to go with us or be part of the group. After returning from breakfast, I walked through the camper to finish up securing everything before the drive home. As I walked by Tom, he grabbed me by the shoulders and turned me toward him. Very seriously and with great intent, he starts telling me how much he loves me and how much he appreciates all that I have done for him over the years, but especially through his illness. I look at him as if to ask, where is all of this coming from? Something in the way he was speaking and the urgency in which he was saying it was making me very uncomfortable. I heard a desperation in his voice as he continued to go on about what he wanted me to do in the future if something were to happen to him. No, I did not want to hear this again. We had already crossed that hurdle a year ago, and I did not want to have this conversation. I assured him that he would be there with me in the future, and I did not want to hear him saying otherwise.

Upon our return home, we made our plans for the trip to Winston on Monday. I was always the one to take Tom to his appointments, but we decided that this time it would be best if his parents took him down. Troy had an IQ test that was going to be administered to all fourth-grade students on Tuesday morning. We knew that if I took his dad down and they ended up keeping him at the hospital, then it would worry him and distract him from doing his best on Tuesday morning. So, the plan was for his parents to take him down on Monday and they would spend the night in a hotel if he ended up having to stay. If he stayed, then on Tuesday morning, I would take Troy to school, and then drive down to be there throughout the rest of his stay and his parents would come back and get Troy from school. So, Troy and I went off to school as usual on Monday morning, and Tom prepared for his trip to Winston. He was scheduled to have his biopsy in the afternoon, so they were planning to leave around noon to drive down. My school was only five minutes from our house, and I had a late morning planning period. For some reason I decided to use it that day to run back home and tell Tom goodbye again, and I would see him early the next morning. He was sitting in a chair when I walked into his parents' house. I leaned over and gave him a big hug and kiss and told him I would be down as soon as I got Troy to school the next morning. It was odd for me not to be going with him, and this was the only time in the past two years I had not been the one to accompany him to his doctor's visits. Tom was admitted, and we talked on the phone later that night for some time and he told me about the tests they had run that day. He did not have any results yet, but hopefully we would know something by the time I got there the next morning. He sounded tired and more winded than usual. I chalked it up to all that he had gone through that day and told him to get some rest. We said, "I love you," and hung up the phone. If only I had known this would be the last time I would ever speak with him.

CHAPTER 15

THE DAY THAT CHANGED EVERYTHING

I awoke around 6:00 am on Tuesday, August 26. I planned to take a shower, pack a few things in an overnight bag, get Troy up and ready for school, drop him off, and then drive down to Tom. As I was about to step into the shower around 6:15, my phone rang. It was a nurse from the hospital telling me that they had found Tom passed out in the bathroom, and I needed to come to the hospital. I told her that I wasn't in Winston and was an hour and a half away. I informed her that his parents were there, and I would call them to come over as quickly as they could, and I would be down as fast as I could get there. I called Tom's parents at the hotel and told them Tom had passed out and they needed to go over to the hospital. My immediate response wasn't total shock or alarm. Prior to the heart transplant, I had been used to receiving calls that Tom had passed out numerous times, and I would have to go back to the hospital. However, fear quickly overtook me, as I realized that this was the first time he had ever passed out with his new heart. What could this mean? I quickly threw the remaining items in my bag and called for Troy to get up. I needed to get him to school so I could start the drive down. I tried to remain calm so that I would not alarm him. As Troy was getting dressed, I took my overnight bag out to the car in the garage. While out of his earshot, I decided to call back down there to see how he was doing and let them know I was on my way. A nurse in his room answered, and I asked her how he was doing. She paused and then said, "I really cannot talk with you about this over the phone; can you please just come here?" I explained to her that I was an hour and a half away, and I was leaving to start the drive down. I also demanded that she tell me what was going on or let me speak with him as I did not want to wait that long to find out how he was doing. She told me that I would need to hang on for a moment. My thoughts were: Hang on? What? Why couldn't she just tell me how he was doing?

By this point, I was getting frustrated with the fact no one wanted to simply tell me how he was or let me talk to him. In a moment, a man's voice came over the phone. It was not the nurse I had been talking with, and immediately my heart began to sink in my chest. I knew something was terribly wrong. He identified himself as the doctor on call and simply stated, "I'm sorry, but your husband has passed. We were not able to revive him, and he passed away at 6:43." I asked him to repeat what he had just said as I was sure that I had misunderstood something. He went on to further explain that Tom had gotten out of bed that morning and went to the bathroom. While in the bathroom, he had pulled the emergency cord. When the nursing staff came to assist him, they found the bathroom door locked. They had to get someone to come and open it, and that is when they found him unresponsive on the floor and pulseless. Code Blue was called, and he was intubated. Resuscitation efforts only resulted in a brief junctional rhythm with pulse and the process was continued until 6:43 at which time it was called, and he was pronounced dead. He went on to let me know that they would be holding his body in the room until I could get down there.

Standing in my garage, I hung up the phone and froze in my tracks for a moment. Shock washed over me like a hand reaching up to clasp my throat. I wanted to scream, yell or cry out. Instead, all that came out of me was a small shaky voice asking myself, "What do I do? How am I going to walk back in that house and tell Troy that his dad died?' I didn't want to take the next step. I wanted time to stop and rewind. This cannot be happening, not now, not after all we have been through. I picked up my phone and called two people. One was my sister. I was going to need her to come and stay with Troy while I went to the hospital. The second one was my friend who happened to be our pastor's daughter. I asked her to please locate her father. I desperately needed him to be there with me when I went in to tell Troy the news. I planned to wait for him to get there before letting him know. I knew that I could not do it alone. That didn't go as I planned though. After making my calls, I walked back into the house from the garage. Troy was sitting at the bar finishing his breakfast. I'm not sure exactly what the look on my face said, but it must have painted a perfect picture for Troy to know what had happened. He looked up at me, and when he saw my face he said, "Daddy died didn't he?" I simply nodded my head up and down, and tears started streaming down my face. He screamed so loudly and we immediately both crumbled to the floor and started hugging and holding each other.

Within five minutes, we heard a knock on our door and our pastor was standing there. Fortunately, when he was called, he was already in our area and arrived quickly at our house. I was so thankful to have him there with us. Soon after, my family and many friends also showed up at our door. It was decided that our pastor and one of Tom's friends would drive me down to the hospital. The rest of my family was going to stay at the house with Troy. Brent was already back in school in Chapel Hill, so they would take care of getting in touch with him as well as any other family members that needed to be notified.

As many times as I had made the trip to Baptist Hospital, this was the longest one I had encountered. Our friend drove us down in his car, and I sat in the back seat while our pastor sat in the passenger's seat in the front. This gave me time to process what I had been told on the phone. I was still in shock and some disbelief. I wanted to get to the hospital to see for myself if this was real. A huge part of me didn't accept it. More questions than answers went through my mind as we drove the ninety minutes to the hospital. How could he have just died? There were so many times over the past year that we almost lost him. He had coded so many times in the hospital before getting his new heart and they always brought him back. He technically died on the operating table when the new heart wouldn't beat and then through the hands of God, the heart started beating on its own when the doctors stepped away. We survived the stem cell transplant. If he had passed during any of these times, it would not have been a surprise, as his condition was always so dire. How then, can he be dead now with a new heart, a stem cell transplant behind him and everything seemingly going so well? This had come out of left field and caught me completely off guard. A year ago, yes, but not now. I also sat there and wrestled with the thoughts of our camping trip the prior weekend. I knew there seemed to be something off with Tom and wondered if he would have gone down on Friday, instead of waiting until Monday would it have made a difference? Why didn't I insist more strongly that we not go camping but instead go to the hospital? He was so adamant that we go ahead with the trip and Monday would be soon enough to get checked. I keep telling myself that I should have won that argument. As I sat in the back seat staring out the window, the thought that kept haunting me the most was that I was not there. If he truly had passed the way the doctor explained it to me on the phone, then he would have died in a bathroom locked behind a door and totally alone. So many times, over the past year, I had raced back to the hospital when I had gotten a call, to be there with him in case he didn't make it. I had slept in a chair numerous nights, afraid to leave the hospital for fear that he would pass, and I would not be there. I rushed back from my father's funeral to be there with him. The one time that I didn't go with him to the hospital or was not close enough to get there quickly and this happens. I simply could not accept this and couldn't wait to get to the hospital to prove that all of this was just a bad dream, and I would walk in and find him there waiting for me.

When we arrived at the hospital, we were taken to a large waiting room on Tom's floor. It did not take long for the reality of what was happening to take hold when I walked into the room. Standing in the room were Tom's parents, who had come over when I called them that morning, his doctors, surgeons, nurses, technicians from the labs, and Sherry. Sherry, who had been our constant contact throughout the entire process of recovery. The person we called whenever any little symptom came up, would answer our endless questions or tell us to get down to the hospital so they could check him. As I walked through the doorway, everyone in the room turned to look at me and with tears streaming down their faces mouthed the words, "I'm sorry!" Suddenly this was becoming very real. The sadness and disbelief in the room was a gray sky with no hint of sunshine. My heart broke again just looking at Tom's parents and knowing what this was doing to them. After hugging and crying with them, Sherry walked over to me and with the utmost despair said, "I am so sorry, I do not know what happened. We are all struggling to understand this." She went on to say that she should have insisted that he come down on Friday when we had called her. Like me, she was wondering if that would have made a difference. I knew that she was blaming herself for not seeing something that apparently was more serious than anyone realized. One by one, the doctors and nurses came by to hug me and tell me how sorry they were and let me know they were in as much shock as I was. Sherry then asked me if I was ready to go see Tom. They had purposely left him in the room until I could get there. Go see Tom? Was I ready for what I was about to do?

We walked down the hall to his room that had been secured. I walked into the room to find him lying there as if he were asleep. He had a peaceful look on his face. Sherry told me she would leave and give me some time with him but would be outside the room if I needed her. Suddenly, like a lightning bolt, the realization that he was truly gone entrenched me. I had no choice but to believe it now. Here he was before me cold and lifeless. I picked up his hand and asked him, "What happened? Why did you leave me now?" I wanted to understand why and how he could suddenly just be gone after all that we had successfully endured. I told him how sorry I was that I was not there. It was devastating me that he had died alone with no one by his side. I laid my head across his chest as I had done so many times before and poured my heart out to him. Only this time, his hand didn't come up to rub my hair to assure me that everything would be OK. Gone was the man who had always calmed my anxiety over the past two years as we had battled this illness. How was I supposed to get through this without him here to support and guide me? I quietly left his room after several minutes shaken to my core and shattered beyond anything that I had ever experienced.

CHAPTER 16

GOING HOME – WITHOUT TOM

Before leaving the hospital, Sherry asked if we would like an autopsy performed. This was something that I wanted so we would know exactly what caused Tom to pass out that morning and ultimately lose his life --- a life that we had worked so long and hard to preserve. After talking with Sherry, I knew that she and the doctors also wanted answers. His death had come as a complete blow to everyone. They too needed to understand what went wrong and if there was anything that could have been done to prevent it. I gave permission for the autopsy, and we went home. We called the funeral home where Tom had already planned his funeral the year before. They would come to the hospital to pick him up and proceed with his plans. This time going home was different from all the other times we had left the hospital. I was alone. Tom's journey would take a different path. There wasn't a jubilant crowd waiting to celebrate good news and share in our happiness. Instead, there was a crowd of family and friends with sorrowful faces and tear-stained eyes.

Just like he planned, we had his services at our church. There was a three-hour visitation before the funeral, and a constant stream of people walked through giving their condolences. Over 600 people attended the funeral as his death sent shock waves throughout our small community. Our pastor spoke about Tom and his incredible journey and how he knew that he was in a better place. The ladies Tom chose sang their beautiful hymns. As all of this was going on around me, what I remember are the emotions raging inside me. I experienced denial that this was even happening, anger that he had just left us, fear and anxiety over what the future would hold, and sadness beyond explanation. I became like a numb statue as people walked by and shook my hand. As our pastor and others spoke, their words became a giant flood washing over me, and I was drowning. At the end of the service, at Tom's request in his funeral plans, the pastor offered an altar call to anyone who would like to come and give their heart to Jesus. Just like the day he gave his testimony one month earlier, the altar was lined with people giving their life to Christ. As we closed his service and I watched people line the altar, the statement that Tom made to me after his testimony raced through my mind. "If even one person comes to know Christ because of what I have gone through, then it was all worth it." I knew that Tom was smiling down from heaven.

After the service we took Tom to his final resting place at the family cemetery. As I laid my single rose across his casket before I walked away, the feeling of absence and enduring grief purged through my soul. Gone was the man who I had loved for 18 years. With him went the loss of our family, the loss of our shared history, and the loss of the future that we had planned together.

CHAPTER 17

THE AUTOPSY

It was Monday, September the 8th, when I received the first news of what had happened to Tom. Although we still did not have the entire autopsy report back yet, Sherry sent me an email outlining what they knew at that time. The primary cause of his death was thought to be severe graft vasculopathy, also called cardiac allograft vasculopathy (CAV), combined with severe pulmonary amyloidosis, pulmonary edema and hyperemia. We had assumed that his death was probably a result of heart rejection only to find out that was not the case. His heart rejection activity was listed as a 1A, which is mild and would not likely have caused him to pass out. My first question to Sherry was what is graft vasculopathy? I asked her to explain it to me in simple terms. She said that instead of the body rejecting the heart which would be considered a heart rejection, that sometimes the arteries reject the heart. It is almost like they wake up and realize that this is the heart that they are not used to working with and the arteries basically become narrow and start blocking blood flow. A more detailed explanation would be that during a heart transplant, the surgeon connects the new heart to the blood vessels and removes the old heart. The new heart is attached by sewing the blood vessels together, creating a graft that allows blood flow to and from the heart. However, complications can arise with the arteries in the transplanted heart, and they may thicken and harden over time. This can occur in approximately 15 to 20% of transplant recipients. During a heart transplantation, the innervation of the heart is partially severed. Due to this graft denervation, patients seldom show classic symptoms of chest pain or pressure, and the first sign of anything being wrong is heart failure or sudden cardiac death. This is especially the case in the first year after transplantation. Since he had clear heart biopsies or only some mild rejection, the fact that this was going on with the arteries was unbeknown to all of us. This helped explain the lower energy he was feeling in the couple of weeks leading up to his death. This explained why he didn't feel like he could walk up that hill to ride that ride with Troy the weekend before his death. Basically, his arteries were closing up and he was not getting enough oxygen. Then on Tuesday morning, when he got up to go to the bathroom, they totally blocked causing him to pass out and ultimately die from cardiac arrest. I was assured that there was nothing that they could have done to prevent this or anything that would have postponed his demise.

The most surprising part of the email was that they found amyloidosis in his lungs and an abnormal amount of fluid buildup in his lungs. When I did receive the final autopsy report, pulmonary amyloidosis was listed as one of the causes of death. His new heart did not show any amyloid, so did the stem cell transplant work to slow down production as planned, or did his body decide to start depositing it in his lungs instead of his heart? This would also help further explain the lack of energy and being short of breath those last two weeks. We will never know for sure when it attacked his lungs, but I know that when I read that, I was so thankful that he never had to know it was in his lungs as well. This man had been through so much with the involvement of his heart and nervous system. A big part of me was relieved that he never had to know or experience any effects of what would have happened as his lungs became stiff with amyloid.

REFLECTIONS

Looking back over that weekend before Tom's death and thinking about his behavior, I think Tom knew he was dying. I believe he knew that something was very off in his body. He had been doing so well since his transplants and then suddenly he was not. He pushed so hard for us to go on that camping trip to Pigeon Forge. He knew that if he had gone to the hospital on Friday instead of waiting until Monday, then he may have missed that one last weekend to spend time with us. I do not think it was a coincidence that he and Troy ended up having the pool all to themselves that Saturday afternoon. He was so happy that they were able to share that special time together. When he stopped me in the camper on Sunday to tell me again about what he wanted me to do if he passed, he knew then that might be his last chance to share his heartfelt wishes and feelings with me. When I walked out of the camper on Sunday morning and saw him sitting at the picnic table staring off into the sky, I think he was reflecting and making peace with the fact that he was not going to be totally healed here on this earth.

Throughout Tom's illness, as I have written, I was always so worried that he would pass, and I would not be there. I was racked with guilt the day he died that I was not by his side. However, as time passed, I realized that Tom died exactly as he wanted to die. He had often told me that he never wanted to die at home or where Troy or I could see him. He stated that he didn't want us to have that memory of him dying or having to call an ambulance. I came to make peace with the fact that I was not meant to be there. I knew that if Tom had chosen how he went, it would have been exactly as it happened.

The events over those two years changed my perspective on many things, and I learned some valuable lessons about the trials of life through which we must pass. I learned that there is no right or wrong way to mourn. In the beginning, grief felt constant. I would love to be able to say that I never blamed God, However that would not be true. I went through a brief period of being angry at Tom and God. I was angry at Tom for leaving me. I was angry that he made us go on that camping trip instead of going to the hospital. I was angry until I got the autopsy back and discovered it would not have mattered and his death was imminent. Then the fact that we went on the camping trip became a priceless treasure. I was angry at God for taking him when he did. I remember asking him over and over, "Why, God, why?" Why didn't you take him all those months when he was lying in a hospital bed only a whisper away from death? Why did you start that heart on the operating table to then snatch it away? Why did you let us survive two transplants and come back home with the hope of a future before us? For a time, I found it hard to pray or feel anything. I was just taking care of business and moving through the motions of life. It was hard to see the light when I was in the thicket of grief. I soon discovered that God could handle my emotions and even my anger. I came to realize that Tom's death did not catch God off guard and was neither meaningless nor without purpose. After I worked through the anger stage of grief, I came to realize that God actually gave us a gift. He did give us a new heart. He did start that heart that day on the operating table when the doctors could not get it to start. He heard the prayers of the people that were sending them up in His name. God allowed Tom to live that day so that he could come back home. He came back home and celebrated one last Christmas with his family. He went to the beach and walked along the ocean and breathed the salty air. He went on camping trips and laughed with family and friends as he sat around the campfire. He shared his last birthday with a community that had supported him throughout his journey and was able to express his gratitude for all they had done. God had added over 23 million seconds for us to be together, and my anger was replaced with thankfulness that He granted us that extra time to have as a family and make memories that will be with us for a lifetime.

As the months passed, the painful emotions came in waves. Sadness, anger, anxiety and a mixture of other emotions would come and go. I would laugh one minute thinking about a joke Tom told or a special memory we shared and then feel guilty for even laughing. I would burst out in tears in a grocery store, as I ran across his favorite gum and then remembered I no longer needed to buy it for him. Grief is unquestionably painful and does not have a specific timeline. Life moves on and you have no choice but to move on with it. The grief has never "gone away," and I know that it never will. However, it did change over the years, and the waves of intense emotions got fewer and farther apart. Sometime after Tom passed, someone gave me this analogy of losing a loved one. Imagine losing one of your arms. You would go through the rest of your life missing that arm and still wishing it were there. However, you learn to adapt and make the necessary adjustments needed to function with only one arm. Grief is like that; you never stop missing that person or wishing they were still there, but you move through life and find a way to live again.

Romans 8:28 says that all things work together for good, for those that love the Lord, according to his purpose. I came to understand that I would never know God's reasons for everything that goes on. No matter how hard I cried or how many times I asked, I never received a definite answer for my "Why?" Instead, God assured me, through his still small voice, that he would walk beside me and never leave or forsake me. He sees the entire picture, whereas we are only looking through a small lens. The people that were impacted by Tom's story and the lives that were changed around the altar were part of God's plan for the greater good. The Bible reminds us that no matter what we face in this life, we can "count it all joy." The joy is not because we are experiencing pain or difficult circumstances, but because we can rest assured that in God's hands, nothing will be wasted. He will comfort, strengthen and hold us up when we are weak. He had held me up so many times over the two years we battled Tom's illness, and I had no doubt that he would continue to do so.

We moved on after Tom's death. It was what he wanted us to do. There isn't a day that goes by that I don't think about him. Thankfully, it is now more with a smile than a tear. I have felt his presence around me so many times over the years, and I see him every time I look into his son's eyes.

The worst pain we have experienced in this life and the comfort we have received may be what someone else needs to hear. 2 Corinthians 1:4 tells us that we can comfort others with a comfort that we have received from God. Everyone suffers somehow; it may be chronic pain, cancer, a broken relationship, disability, or simply a struggle with sin in your life. It is my hope and prayer that if you are reading our story, you come to realize that suffering can be one of the greatest instruments in God's hands to help you realize your ultimate dependence on Him and that your ultimate hope rests in Him alone. Tom never allowed his suffering to become an excuse to focus on himself. Rather, he allowed the comfort of Christ to engulf him, and he would want others to know that Christ's strength is strong enough for their weakness, their pain and their suffering.

The song "Heaven Changes Everything," by Big Daddy Weave, contains the following lyrics, and I will close our story with this: "A goodbye would be goodbye with no I'll see you again. And when a life is over, that would simply be the end, Thank you Jesus. Heaven changes everything." We love you Tom, and we will see you again very soon!

My precious Raggedy Ann
with her wooden heart.

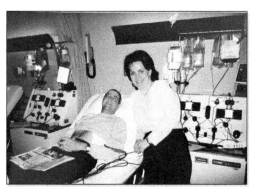
Stem Cell Transplant

Giving Our Testimony

Our last camping trip and
two days before his death.

Printed in the USA
CPSIA information can be obtained
at www.ICGtesting.com
LVHW010848200924
791521LV00012B/566